NEW DIRECTIONS
FOR
PHILANTHROPIC
FUNDRAISING

Dwight F. Burlingame, Timothy L. Seiler,
Eugene R. Tempel
Indiana University Center on Philanthropy
EDITORS

WOMEN AS FUNDRAISERS

THEIR EXPERIENCE IN AND INFLUENCE ON AN EMERGING PROFESSION

Julie C. Conry
Ohio State University Health Sciences Center

EDITOR

D1114534

NUMBER 19, SPRING 1998

WOMEN AS FUNDRAISERS: THEIR EXPERIENCE IN AND INFLUENCE ON AN EMERGING PROFESSION
Julie C. Conry (ed.)
New Directions for Philanthropic Fundraising, No. 19, Spring 1998
Dwight F. Burlingame, Timothy L. Seiler, Eugene R. Tempel, Editors

NEW DIRECTIONS FOR PHILANTHROPIC FUNDRAISING is indexed in Higher Education Abstracts and Philanthropic Index.

Microfilm copies of issues and articles are available in 16 mm and 35 mm, as well as microfiche in 105 mm, through University Microfilms Inc., 300 North Zeeb Road, Ann Arbor, Michigan 48106-1346.

ISSN 1072-172X   ISBN 0-7879-4268-5

NEW DIRECTIONS FOR PHILANTHROPIC FUNDRAISING is part of The Jossey-Bass Nonprofit Sector Series and is published quarterly by Jossey-Bass Inc., Publishers, 350 Sansome Street, San Francisco, California 94104-1342.

SUBSCRIPTIONS cost $67.00 for individuals and $115.00 for institutions, agencies, and libraries. Prices subject to change. Refer to the Ordering Information page at the back of this issue.

EDITORIAL CORRESPONDENCE should be sent to the editor, Dwight F. Burlingame, Center on Philanthropy, Indiana University, 550 West North Street, Suite 301, Indianapolis, IN 46202-3162.

www.josseybass.com

Printed in the United States of America on acid-free recycled paper containing 100 percent recovered waste paper, of which at least 20 percent is postconsumer waste.

Contents

Editor's Notes

FEW THEMES are as prominent in contemporary fundraising today as that of transition. Attend any professional fundraising conference, scan the book titles, or survey the Internet dialogue, and it is evident that discussion invariably centers on the rapidly changing landscape within the nonprofit sector. Change is omnipresent, and how to cope with it, manage it, anticipate it, and, ultimately, conquer it is the topic of the hour. Changes in regulation, technology, demographics, volunteerism, and donor behaviors preoccupy practitioners and constantly demand new modes of thinking about and approaching old problems.

Within the last decade alone, one of the most striking changes in fundraising has been the composition of the workforce itself—the dramatic increase in the numbers of women choosing and pursuing fundraising careers. Women now make up the majority of memberships (roughly 52 to 60 percent) in the three major professional organizations representing fundraisers: the Council for the Advancement and Support of Education (CASE), the National Society of Fund Raising Executives (NSFRE), and the Association for Healthcare Philanthropy (AHP). Women occupy all fundraising job categories, in some specialty areas holding upwards of 65 percent of the positions. They are employed by a vast and diverse matrix of nonprofit institutions and organizations: health care, education, social services, environmental causes, the arts, churches, and synagogues. They play key roles in campaigns and have established, either formally or informally, large networks and associations for women fundraisers, philanthropists, and volunteers.

In ten years' time, these marked shifts in the gender make-up and workplace culture of fundraising have produced both opportunity and challenge. For practitioners and the organizations and

NEW DIRECTIONS FOR PHILANTHROPIC FUNDRAISING, NO. 19, SPRING 1998 © JOSSEY-BASS PUBLISHERS

institutions they represent, diversity, professionalization, and feminization trends are issues that will be prominent as the occupation of fundraising continues to evolve. In a field known for blending art and science, fundraisers are facing a clear time of transition and redefinition in their professional lives.

The values inherent in the nonprofit sector—altruism, relationship-centered work, service to society, and affiliation with mission-centered organizations—continue to be strong occupational draws that bring women into paid fundraising roles. And as the 1990s draw to a close, multiple pressures mount for nonprofits to significantly augment annual budgets with private contributions. The demand for competent, experienced, and talented fundraisers has reached an all-time high. Performance expectations are equally high. But even though altruism and service still count as key values, making effective use of available resources to reach fundraising goals is as crucial in the nonprofit sector as it is in the for-profit culture. Within nonprofits, any fundraising position now requires the practitioner to not only successfully raise funds—that is a given—but to demonstrate management skills, leadership, marketing acumen, technological sophistication, and mastery of all modes of communication. Much is being asked, and keen competitive forces are testing both the elders and the apprentices who need to learn from them.

This volume—*Women as Fundraisers*—was compiled, in large part, to examine, address, and analyze some of the most compelling aspects of the last decade's gender changes in the fundraising workforce and workplace culture. The discussions in these chapters range from the pragmatic to the philosophical. With rich detail, the authors use personal histories, demographic trends, statistical data, and life and work experiences to highlight some of the significant ways the nonprofit sector has been and is now being shaped by women's leadership in fundraising and greater participation in the professional ranks. The cases analyzed and scenarios presented provide contrasts that are, at times, striking. Further, these essays present a departure point for debate and discussion that is intended to provoke more questions than answers, to inspire more inquiry, and to spark new levels of awareness.

In Chapter One, Martha A. Taylor, who has devoted significant efforts during most of her professional career to increasing the knowledge base about women and philanthropy, outlines a number of strategies to develop both professional success and personal satisfaction in a fundraising career. Her perspective as manager, fundraiser, and mentor provides unique insights into the daily dilemmas of fundraising and balancing professional demands and personal commitments. Her guidelines for navigating organizational barriers and developing credibility within and outside an institution are built from years of experience. It is also her belief that the opportunities available now for women in fundraising to initiate and forge coalitions with women philanthropists have never been better, or more promising, for both groups.

In Chapter Two, Sondra Shaw-Hardy looks at the career paths, life choices, and professional achievements of five women development executives—vice presidents and CEOs—who speak candidly about their work and the inherent challenges in assuming top leadership positions in fundraising. How their values, experiences, educational backgrounds, and personal visions have influenced their leadership styles and philosophies is indicative of the breadth, depth, and innovation women are bringing to the highest levels of fundraising management. All have to some degree shattered a glass ceiling to attain executive status, and as pathfinders they continue to focus on the future of fundraising as a profession.

Keeping within the theme of professional development and building career success, in Chapter Three, Phyllis S. Fanger recounts the creation, growth, and development of one of this country's first, and now largest, organizations of women advancement professionals. As a founding member of the Boston-based Women in Development (WID) group, Fanger was one of the primary architects of a grassroots gathering that became an eight-hundred-member organization. With a mission to foster a climate within fundraising in which women can achieve and succeed, WID evolved from an informal network of nine individuals into a comprehensive association with extensive mentoring, education, and networking programs. As a replicable model, WID is clearly a prototype for others seeking proven ways to advance the success rates of women in fundraising careers.

Chapter Four's focus is my own examination of the current status of women within fundraising as measured by compensation rates and organizational position. It is what I characterize as a good-news-bad-news scenario, that is, the data indicate that the growth in numbers of women fundraisers has been tempered by persistent pay gaps and slow and uneven professional advancement. Women holding senior management positions in fundraising are still a fraction of their overall numbers as a group, and salary equity too often remains an elusive ideal rather than a guaranteed component of career advancement. It is a complex problem that defies simple explanations. But as fundraising continues its shift toward a predominantly female workforce, these issues will require sustained attention for some time to come.

The status of women in fundraising and volunteer roles within traditional organizations and institutions is also central to Chapters Five and Six. Within religious institutions, as Jennifer M. Goins and Janette E. McDonald point out, the radically changing role of women in American society has had a profound impact on the organizational structures of religious fundraising, particularly on groups that historically built programs on the volunteer efforts of women. It is a pivotal time in history, they believe, for women to move into more visible leadership roles in trusteeships within religious organizations and exert greater influence in fundraising and in setting direction and policy. Similarly, Chapter Six details just such a model within a traditionally female-centered nonprofit—the YWCA. Executive director of the Columbus (Ohio) YWCA, Karen Schwarzwalder, outlines an ambitious fundraising campaign agenda in which the first decision made was to assemble an all-woman campaign leadership team. Although it was a "first" in the community, this exclusive partnership of women has been cited frequently as playing a major part in the campaign's success.

In the final two chapters of this volume, the pragmatic and the personal merge in two reflective essays. In "Why Diversity Matters," Margaret A. Hendricks speaks to a number of significant issues—political, organizational, and personal—that coincide with the changing face of today's workplace. And champion volunteer, philanthropist, and fundraiser Madelyn M. Levitt shares, in Chapter Eight, her guiding principles for the many roles she plays to advance the mission of higher education, and the status of women philanthropists, fundraisers, and volunteers. At age seventy-three, she is chairing her second consecutive multimillion-dollar campaign for Drake University in Des Moines, Iowa, which is some distance from her first fundraising efforts to sell Girl Scout cookies during the Great Depression. That task shaped her lifetime philosophy: To be the best at whatever you strive for, you must always go that extra mile.

In compiling this volume, the contributors embraced a complex topic with considerable thought and unflagging enthusiasm. In the midst of their busy professional and personal lives, each made a singular commitment to share their unique perspectives, in effect, to enrich the written history of women in the nonprofit sector and document their achievements as well as their struggles. I thank them for giving so freely of that commodity we all need more of—their time—as well as their patience with the editing process. It has been a tremendous experience to collaborate with each of them and to learn from their life's work and wisdom.

Julie C. Conry
Editor

JULIE C. CONRY *is director of development, The Ohio State University Health Sciences Center/College of Nursing. A graduate of Oberlin College and former Kiplinger Fellow at Ohio State, she writes, lectures, and conducts workshops and seminars on nonprofit fundraising issues, proposal development, and corporate and foundation giving.*

To be successful and satisfied as a woman in development, you first must determine your philosophical base, discover your passion for your cause, and define your philanthropic values.

1

Women development officers: Finding success and satisfaction in a career of service

Martha A. Taylor

FINDING SUCCESS AND SATISFACTION as a woman development officer involves three aspects: establishing your personal philosophical base in philanthropy; becoming proficient in technical skills, and being aware of special challenges for women; and initiating a powerful coalition with philanthropists, especially women. And successful women in development must be passionate about their causes.

Women have discovered development as a caring profession in which they can make a great contribution to society. Development is a call to service, as Henry Rosso (1996) puts it so aptly, and is a return to the first profession open to women in the United States—charitable work. Women now make up about 50 to 60 percent of the development profession. They have great capabilities in this field, and it is one in which they can contribute to making the world a better place for their children.

NEW DIRECTIONS FOR PHILANTHROPIC FUNDRAISING, NO. 19, SPRING 1998 © JOSSEY-BASS PUBLISHERS

The case examples, quotes, and stories in this chapter are all from anonymous sources. Because many of the events described were sensitive, some of the women did not even want the type of their institution mentioned, some for fear that their institution or they themselves could be identified. Francie Ostrower (1995) found that that kind of guarantee of anonymity enabled philanthropists to speak openly in her book *Why the Wealthy Give*. So despite the anonymity of the sources, the examples in this chapter provide positive guidance that can benefit others in the development profession.

The philosophical base

Development is a call to service. The most difficult task you will have in your career as a development officer is to determine your own personal philanthropic vision. Only by being philanthropic yourself will you be able to help others in their philanthropy. Empowering yourself to be a philanthropist is what sets apart the soul of the outstanding development officer and leader.

Being a philanthropist is giving time and money to the causes you care about, and supporting your own organization financially is essential. Many in our field subscribe to the "5/5 goal" advanced in a public service ad campaign a number of years ago: give 5 percent of income annually and 5 hours per week of volunteer time to improve your community (Wuthnow and Hodgkinson, 1990, p. 305). Others have a goal of tithing—giving 10 percent. Another idea is to give a deferred gift, such as a bequest to an organization in your will.

Being a role model in giving is extremely difficult because of the job demands and societal expectations for development officers. People tend to think our titles mean we receive large paychecks, which is not usually the case. The compensation of a vice president at a nonprofit is far less than that of a vice president in a corporation, but the costs of wardrobe and travel are similar. Despite these barriers, women must be strong donors and serve on visible boards.

We must be role models. And we must be passionate about the causes we are raising money for.

Almost all development officers take jobs for organizations in which they believe. Your appeals to donors are all the more compelling if you have a personal reason for being employed at your organization—a personal connection.

Another essential part of your philosophical base is the realization that you are an educator of philanthropy—a counselor. You will be involved with individuals in some of the most sensitive and personal conversations in their lives—conversations about the disposition of their assets and how that reflects their values and life. This trusting, close relationship is the basis of the philanthropic partnership model.

The two contemporary models of development officers are the *philanthropic partnership builder* (PPB) and the *technocrat fundraiser* (TFR). Some development operations have moved to the TFR approach totally, believing that business, sales, and marketing techniques can be applied to development. The TFRs view donors as prospects and targets. They are evaluated on a moves-management system taken to the extreme—a system in which staff are compensated by the number of moves they make on a prospect. TFRs move from institution to institution, and many practice "slash and burn" fundraising. Money is requested from people in order to make quotas and campaign goals—thus burning out the donors. Unfortunately, European fund development started on a partnership model but is now resembling the TFR model, if the titles of articles in a recent journal are any indication (Pyne and Robertson, 1997).

The PPBs view themselves as philanthropists first. They view their job as a calling. Many have risen through the ranks of an organization because of their commitment to a cause. The PPB model is the basis of our profession and furnishes the model that will serve us best. Organizations that use the PPB model are in the long term the most successful in raising money. The PPB model is returning once more as the most successful, and it is clearly the model women donors desire. But many women development officers find themselves as PPBs within a TFR organization. My own success and that of the UW (University of Wisconsin) Foundation is the result of our subscribing to the PPB model. Our role is to work with people as a partner to solve the problems of society, to perpetuate values to the next generation, and to further the education of our leadership for future generations.

The philanthropic partnership builder works to identify donors' total charitable interests and includes those in all discussions. If the donor's wishes cannot be carried out by the partnership builder's organization, the donor is made aware of another organization or cause that can accommodate those wishes.

PPB development officers must educate, teach, and minister to people whose incomes are often ten times higher than their own. You, as a PPB, must be able to go into someone's extravagant home and talk to that person about his or her life and then drive down to the trailer park to talk to an older man about a deferred gift. And the man in the trailer park may very well give much more than the person in the extravagant home. A PPB development officer values each donor as a person, with his or her own distinct values and interests.

Wealth can isolate people from one another. Charitable giving permits psychological self-actualization, humanism, or a sense of connection to a greater power. People are searching for the reasons they are here on this earth, and our job is to help with the search. As a philanthropic partnership builder, you know that people cannot give money away until they feel valued personally, know who they are, and know what their lives mean. You can help your donors decide what they want to accomplish. If you are a philanthropic partner, your donors will call you to seek your advice when they want to give money.

Practicalities and personal aspects

Once your personal philosophy and passion for the cause are identified, learning the technical aspects of development is the next step. But for female development officers, there are a few additional personal considerations.

Barriers for women in development

Twenty-five years ago a woman entering the field of development might never have had the opportunity to even think about a job in planned giving, major gifts, or management. Now that the glass ceiling in development is being broken, many women are pursuing positions in major and planned gifts at both the junior and senior development levels. A woman's ability to understand planned giving is no longer in question. But in the past, men were proprietary about planned giving jobs because these positions were better paid and were more likely to lead to career advancement. Even when women were hired for major gift positions, they frequently found that men hoarded the good prospects and turned entry-level donors over to women staff members. However, in fairness, prospect hoarding is not entirely gender-specific; in most organizations, the best prospects traditionally are managed by senior development officers. Two decades ago, those senior people were usually men, whereas many of the junior professionals were women.

Twenty-five years ago, discrimination against women in certain roles came from both men and women. One illustration of this involved a colleague who was asked to put together a brochure for a financial planning seminar. The graphic designer used a photo of a woman in a dark business suit teaching a class. The development officer's boss reacted by saying, "We can't use that picture because too many of our clients won't accept a woman in a financial role." This was a blow to the woman, who had hoped to move into major gift work; the remark revealed her boss's attitude toward a woman in that role. Now with so many women in trust offices and the financial industry, that image is changing.

Another organization planned a day for "corporate wives." The wives were given a tour of the child care facility and the art center in town, while their husbands determined the future of the organization in a business meeting. A female staff member complained: "Why don't you invite the women to the business meeting? They are thinking individuals." She received a two-page memo from her male boss stating, "If you knew corporate wives like I know corporate wives you would not even suggest such a thing. They are interested in family matters."

The wonderful irony of this story is that now this woman—who is a development vice president—does know corporate wives a lot better than her former boss does. She knows that many corporate husbands have gotten ahead in their careers because of their smart and extremely capable corporate wives.

Attitudes toward women donors

Often, women development officers face problems when there is discrimination against women donors within their organizations. One colleague told me she was asked to call and thank a woman who had given $10,000 to her nonprofit—because she herself was a woman. The donor said, "If I were a man and gave $10,000, the president would have called me. I know you are a nice person, but I can tell you are very young and probably not in a senior position. Your organization does not value women." How many women have we offended because the development office did not have a senior executive contact them?

The language of development is male-oriented. The "campaign" is from a military model. To "solicit" someone has been used in a context that is derogatory toward women. The Council for Advancement and Support of Education uses a male term for its most highly rated speakers: *heavy hitters.* The sports analogy falls short on some women. We need a new model for development that recognizes the importance of women as donors and development officers (Addams, 1910).

Overcoming the challenges for women in development

Women have advanced a long way in development over the past twenty-five years, but the challenges remain: salary differences between men and women, position achieved within the organiza-tion, advancement into management, and access to major prospects. Several women interviewed for this chapter cited communication in meetings as an area of difficulty. One woman pointed out that indeed if she, a senior manager, presents an idea in a meeting, she is not heard as a male peer would be. I hope male colleagues will be sensitive to this common complaint from female colleagues, even colleagues in the management circle.

Whom you report to was another issue of concern raised by several women. One woman said, "In my first position I reported to a woman and *loved* it. One could sit in any position and need not worry about body language. In all subsequent positions, I have reported to a man. Two men I have worked for had problems with women, and I believe this will always be an issue for women."

Several women raised another issue about whom they reported to. Does their boss give them access to the person above? One woman in charge of development reported to an academic dean who guarded access to the dean. The woman could never make contact with the dean without going through the associate dean. Neither dean was knowledgeable about fundraising and, consequently, she believed they never raised nearly the amount they should have. She advises, "Never take a development position unless you have access to the individual who can make decisions on programs major donors will support. Chances are you won't be taken very seriously unless you report directly to the CEO."

She added, "One of the important parts of a development officer's job is to brief the nonprofit's representative before each visit and critique them afterward. It is very difficult to have this responsibility without the authoritative position to go with it. Many male CEOs are strongly influenced by title and will listen better to a vice president than to a director of development that works for their vice president."

Two women managers believed they needed the credibility of overseeing a separate foundation, as well as being the chief development officer. As women, they believed the extra clout helped give them credibility.

In today's competitive environment, building a development portfolio requires a continual effort to recognize career opportunities and take risks in pursuing them.

Women should pursue major and planned giving. Major and planned gifts are now key areas of advancement because they are the center of development work. The best background for individuals in development management is major gift and campaign work. The CEO must be a development officer first. With more women seeking major gifts, more women donors will be asked, and their priorities will begin to affect organizations and institutions. If a woman proves herself and her ability to ask for money, she will advance in this field, and certainly those credentials are needed for management.

Access to money brings power and prestige. Some women professionals view power as negative. Much literature and numerous workshops have focused on encouraging women to accept power and use it in a positive way. For those with spiritual roots, the word *power* comes from a religious base, and it does not refer to the person's power. The person is just a vehicle to use the power for good. Visible access to money brings the most power to development officers. If you have good relationships with donors who have wealth and influence, you will be a most valuable person to your organization.

Women should keep focused on the top twenty prospects. Make sure you communicate with them quarterly. Senior women in development at large institutions should have multimillion-dollar prospects.

I advocate a prospect system whereby all staff people have access to all prospects unless there is some compelling reason not to have the contact. Access to prospective donors is not just an issue for a large institution. At a cultural organization, a senior woman who was responsible for development could not have access to the major prospects. The male president insisted he should see these people himself. Would this situation have existed if the development director had been a man? The senior woman believes that if she had been a man, she would have had access to the prospects. You, as a development officer, must be aware of your prospect base and your access to the major and megagifts for your organization.

Women should be visible role models in development. Despite all the progress made by women, they are still often left out of public, visible roles. One colleague at a large, coed educational institution said that she is very happy to have women and philanthropy programs developing because finally she has an opportunity to make a public presentation to donors.

At a dedication ceremony of a major basketball arena at a large educational institution, there were no women speakers on the agenda. Only male donors and university representatives were invited to speak. The woman whose department raised all the money for the basketball arena was silent about promoting herself as a speaker. Where were the other women who could have offered her name?

Women should be role models for other women. Having women mimic men's traditional work habits is a one-dimensional working model. Women need to be role models as working mothers who can introduce innovation, such as part-time schedules, into the workplace without sacrificing career growth. And women must mentor other women in their struggles. Suffice it to say that women must also be keenly aware of the allocation of resources for their use: support staff, office space and quality, travel arrangements, and budget. Mentors who will advocate for a woman in an institution can greatly help with these issues. Women should learn from mentors and welcome educational opportunities. It is important to have both male and female mentors. In particular, it is imperative for women to have several women mentors—in addition to women's professional organizations. Women should also find donors who will mentor them. In exchange, these donors and volunteers can be given information that will be helpful to them in succeeding as women on the board.

Women should seek to build friendships with women colleagues and donors. Women will naturally know to connect to male colleagues and bosses who, in most organizations, hold the power. Touching base and communicating with women and men in the workplace is very different. One Wall Street financier who works in a male-dominated environment said she was told by a consultant to call men up or drop by their offices just to touch base, quickly and with a short comment. Women, however, will have long bonding conversations but do not need to touch base. They can just pick up where they left off.

Deborah Blum (1997) advocates that women will have power only when other women support them, and she presents examples.

Early women's philanthropic work in this country was successful only when women banded together to accomplish a philanthropic goal. Jane Addams' (1910) work in founding the social reform movement in this nation was made possible only because of collaboration with other women. Karen Blair (1994) points out that early charitable work by women to advance the arts beginning in 1890 was strengthened by arts organizations collaborating with other women's groups.

In the book I wrote with Sondra Shaw (1995), we describe a key point in women's motivations to give: collaboration. Development officers seeking to advance their own position and bring additional funds to the organization must affirm this core factor in women's connection to an organization.

Formal educational opportunities are also essential to advancing in development. These opportunities include conferences, seminars, and degree programs. In the past twenty years, about thirty degree programs have emerged, including the degrees from the Indiana University Center on Philanthropy. If you have the opportunity to pursue a degree in this field, you will find it highly beneficial. I chose the field of development after college and pursued a graduate degree in development before entering employment in the field, which makes my background unusual. A formal education in development gives you the rare opportunity to study trends in the field. The educational experience has benefited me and the organization I serve greatly.

Practical issues and job survival

Women face some special challenges in any career, but the following specific challenges were mentioned by most of the women contacted for this chapter.

Travel

Travel schedules and long hours are extremely challenging in major gift work. Even if you work for a local group, nights and weekends are needed if you are doing the job right. One adage states that you should always catch up on paperwork during off hours or on days when you can't be in contact with donors. You should be using your work time to contact donors.

When you travel, assemble a professional itinerary with everything in the file: contact reports, background information, and directions. Put all of the information on one sheet of paper. And leave a copy for home. Avoid taking brochures about a project or description with you. Go in with just your ideas. Follow up with a written proposal and brochure. The follow-up contact provides another way to be in touch with the person. Development staff can become exhausted by travel schedules. Some organizations allow more flexible hours between campaigns, which is highly desirable. Keeping creativity and enthusiasm alive while meeting with donors is essential to good development. Like other financial professionals, we are not approached simply for technical advice. We must be able to counsel people on some of the most sensitive issues in their lives—issues related to their money.

To help legal professionals avoid burnout from this kind of role, modern management books advocate a two-month sabbatical every seven years (Kuczmanski and Kuczmanski, 1995). First visits with a particular donor can be emotionally draining, and extra time is needed for donors who have become friends. With three or four visits a day, you will keep refreshed and lively—and thus do a better job. The bottom line should be results within three years from the initial contact—not the number of contacts in a day. Know your organization's expectations, but question a system of evaluation that puts emphasis on "moves" rather than relationships. Moves management has gone astray from its once-useful purpose as a tool for development officers. Moves management discriminates against women and our communication styles.

A female colleague is one of the highest producers in the field. She spends at least 50 percent of her time on the road, or getting ready to go on the road. Sometimes it bothers her that because she is unmarried she travels more, whereas people with children stay at home and get paid the same salary. Travel duty deserves more compensation or more time off; it is that demanding. This colleague does not mind the travel; she just wants the organization to appreciate her efforts.

Balancing parenting and development careers

It is very difficult for both parents to have fast-track careers and children too. Even if each parent has a mid-range professional career, great stress is put on marriage, family, and career. Sage advice is to put spouse first, then children. Many couples put children first and hardly see each other alone. At the other extreme is the sad story of a colleague in Iowa who said she never made it to one of her son's football games because she was working. Maybe she didn't like football, but she missed out on a major part of her son's life.

One suggestion from women working in development who have children is to hire as much help as possible when the children are young. One woman said, "Pay for domestic help to ease up your time so you can spend more time with your kids. I found that I could hire babysitters when the children were small, but I cut back on my travel because they were so physically in need of me. I had more time for my career during elementary school years. When they became teenagers, I no longer could hire babysitters, and they really needed me around. I had to cut back on my travel again then."

The key to managing travel is having a fantastic support network, whether it includes husband, female friends, relatives, or other families who will trade driving duties and child care. Always make your scheduling decisions so you can spend more time with your children. This applies even to little time slots, when you really would rather avoid the noise and chaos at home to finish a report for work. In other words, when you are asking, "Should I do this now or go home and be with the family and finish it later at night?," the best choice is to go home.

The ideal organization is one that expects us to churn out the work when we need to but where family is a priority. Flexible hours and part-time hours for family reasons are allowed. At the UW Foundation, there are now three women who are major gift development officers; each holds an 80 percent appointment. The stimulation, flexibility, and diversity of our work—both volunteer and paid—is truly excellent.

Relating to donors

Problems can arise when women (and men) get too close emotionally to donors. The development relationship is not a normal friendship in which both parties enjoy the relationship equally. In some cases, elderly donors are especially lonesome. This is not a gender-specific problem. It is good to befriend donors but not get overly involved. There are differences between a meaningful visit, a friendship, and a situation where a lonely person takes advantage of you. For example, sexual harassment can be problematic in development relationships, and it must be reported immediately. Most women in development can anticipate whether a person will make them uncomfortable and should ask to have that person transferred to someone else.

Sometimes people may try to keep attention riveted on themselves by continuing to be prospects, fearing that once they commit they will be forgotten. To some degree they are correct. We in development are often eager to pursue. Some of us think getting there is half the fun. Remember the importance of stewardship contacts and that the best next donor is a past donor.

Communicating and building relationships

For years, women attended "business communication" seminars that stressed "report talk"—male business talk. Many women had to be taught report talk because their natural tendency was "rapport talk," which is more personal and involves layers of conversation. To most men, report talk comes more naturally. "Sensitive men" know rapport talk—women's style of communication—in which you build upon what the other person says. It is less direct. In my workshops on women and philanthropy, I encourage all development officers—male or female—to use rapport talk with women donors, at least until the communication style of the prospect becomes clear.

A woman development officer needs to master both types of communication. She must be able to do report talk in a board room with men and women and when she meets with primarily male groups to talk about her organization. She also must remember how to communicate with women, many of whom prefer rapport talk.

Relationships with staff and colleagues are critical in development, as in other operations. Relationships with female staff members can sometimes be difficult because women have adopted certain behavior in order to get ahead. As the new CEO of the development operation of a large nonprofit, a woman explained: "When I arrived on the job, the financial officer made my life hell. She told lies about me to her staff, who were responsible for all our gift and data processing. It took me a long time and many sleepless nights to show these people I wasn't the incompetent misfit she portrayed." This same woman had difficulty with another female peer who said malicious things about their male boss. "When I wouldn't participate in this negative discussion, she cut me off and took every opportunity to thwart my projects."

The essence of outstanding major gift development work is relationship building. Some managers in development have not come through the ranks of major gifts but through planned giving; they may have been just a gift "closer." Building a relationship and going on cold calls takes talent. Some men are outstanding in this; some women are weak. By and large, more women are taught good relationship-building skills from childhood.

But a male colleague at a small nonprofit is quick to point out that he is a relationship builder. He secures a great deal of financial support for his organization, but the management has no understanding of or appreciation for his softer, more long-term building style.

This colleague has fortitude, along with the conviction that the best way to build relationships with donors—especially women donors—takes a great deal of time and a different approach. And he lets the bottom line determine his effectiveness.

Unfortunately, both men and women who practice a long-term, relationship-building model of fundraising are often overlooked by their organizations because they are not considered aggressive enough for development work that is based on a sales or marketing model. Now that relationship-building development is once again recognized as the best way to raise money, women will rise to the ranks of major and planned giving officers, and from there into management.

Our goal may be to raise money for projects near to our own hearts or to enable our donors to reach their fullest potential as philanthropists. The great satisfaction in this field is not in closing a gift but in seeing the impact of funding a worthy project to help society—the reason we entered this field in the first place.

Sadly, in the pursuit of money for organizations, nonprofits have raided profit-making organizations for models of success. Sales models may have some good process ideas for us in development, but the underlying concepts and motivations are completely different.

The Indiana University Center on Philanthropy, Women's Philanthropy Institute, National Society of Fund Raising Executives, and the Council for Advancement and Support of Education have been working to reestablish the relationship model in development. With more women entering the field, that model will once again regain its rightful position as the most effective way to raise money and educate the population on philanthropy.

Women philanthropists and development officers

The women's philanthropy movement, which is driven by women donors, has had a great deal to do with women's rise in the development profession. In addition, a coalition of women philanthropists and women development officers will provide opportunities to form strategic alliances that bring great resources to an organization, as well as new priorities in some cases. This coalition will also result in personal fulfillment and friendship for both parties.

Women donors are the greatest audience for philanthropy in the next century. Women now control 60 percent of the nation's investment wealth and make up 43 percent of the nation's wealthiest individuals. There is a powerful, religiously based constituency of women who live frugal, quiet lives and leave the bulk of their estate to nonprofits. It is essential for women in development to learn to work with and partner with women philanthropists.

Too often, organizations will plead that there are no women available to be on their board. When Carol Toussaint, a consultant in volunteer leadership, hears that excuse, she sends the group a list of qualified women. Her advocacy has been so effective that the state of Wisconsin and the University of Wisconsin–Madison assembled a computer database on women with the credentials to serve on corporate and nonprofit boards.

The woman development officer who works with women donors will advance because she will be successful in gaining new money and resources for her institution. Working with women will take more time, but the results will be there. Some young women do not see the potential of women donors. One young development officer was standing in line at an NSFRE (National Society of Fund Raising Executives) conference and overheard Sondra Shaw and me talking about our new book on women as philanthropists. She said, "I'm not interested in women donors. I call on men—they have the money; they make the decisions." Shaw and I found this idea prevalent among many young women development officers and among many men of all ages. Planned giving officers are the exception. They know most of their prospects will be women, many of whom will be widows.

Yes, perhaps in some couples the man makes the philanthropic decision. But in how many households does the woman make the decision? No data exist to answer the question. Most philanthropic gifts by couples are joint decisions, that is, the couple identifies their causes based on the interests of both partners. Put 100 percent of your effort into cultivating both members of a married couple and assume that their decisions are joint ones until you receive other information.

The bottom line for women development officers is this: Look at women as a great potential audience from which to solicit new gifts, and learn to ask women. Some new models of fundraising are based on women's psychology and giving patterns. However, remember that there are wide differences among women and even greater differences among women of different generations.

One problem becomes apparent in a coed institution. In the past five years, a number of programs in coed institutions have begun to seek support from women—a movement I have strongly advocated. Yet it is important for women development officers at coed institutions to have duties involving asking both men and women. Keep yourself a generalist. At several institutions that have hired full-time staff dedicated to raising funds from women, those positions are not high in the development office yet. That is not the area of advancement and recognition in the institution—unless the position is devoted solely to raising major gifts. A few senior development officers, myself included, have positions that include the women's program in addition to other duties. Even if you are a young woman development officer taking on a women's program, ask for other duties. You will gain strength and credibility with your ability to ask for money from all people, although you may find the women's program to be the most rewarding activity professionally and personally.

The second benefit of the coalition of women philanthropists and women development officers is the number of strategic alliances you can create for institutional change and advancement. The powerful coalition of women development officers and women philanthropists has developed over the past two decades; in the past decade, it has increased greatly. The future will see more of bridge building. This is an opportunity for women—staff and volunteers—to take on a project with a passion and see what can be accomplished.

Advancing projects of interest to the women at an institution is the first result. Women may be interested in the stereotypical "women's projects," but they may be good political allies to move other projects forward as well. Women have reinvigorated fund drives, both as volunteer leaders and major contributors, for projects to help the environment, arts, family, and education. Women development officers and philanthropists have partnered to raise funds for social service agencies—particularly for poor women and children—and for many other programs that would not have existed otherwise. Women's health, science, history, economics, and athletics are other good examples of programs that will go forward when women philanthropists contribute to them and encourage others—both men and women—to support them. The number of women faculty in higher education will rise as more women philanthropists come into leadership positions.

Women philanthropists have led increases in overall support for institutions. That is the emphasis of most women's programs—to raise the level of giving by women to all purposes at the organization.

Once when a colleague faltered with her new boss, she received good advice: Become allied with the largest donors for the organization, and find some new major donors. This strategy worked.

The partnership of women development officers and women philanthropists means that neither group is ever "left out" of activities again because of their sex. Being left out as a woman in any field is something you must expect and overcome. There is no doubt you are left out of certain gatherings because you are a woman. For years, women have worked to be invited to the mainstream events in the community—the Rotary, for example. Women are joining these groups—ever so slowly—and even more slowly getting their employers to pay their membership dues. Fortunately, women's professional organizations have also been launched and are flourishing. These organizations provide professional networking, as well as the psychological support of other women. Problems women face in the workforce are more manageable if they can be shared with others.

The first woman chair of the UW Foundation board, Jean Manchester Biddick, was a retired businesswoman accustomed to working mostly with men—and to not being included in discussions about sharing rides, playing golf, or going to athletic events. She was a strong, quiet leader who mentored me and many other women; she helped us succeed in a male environment. She had worked in a male environment and been mentored by—and then mentored—men. Yet her strongest friendships were in the women's professional organizations she helped to found in our city.

The nonprofit world is where the next great advances will be made by women as volunteer leaders and development professionals. I have a dream of one day organizing a national conference for women who are campaign and philanthropic leaders. Someday such a conference will occur because it will only be with this powerful coalition of women philanthropists and women development officers that change will really take place in our society. This coalition will bring about the change in the social fabric that is desired by men and women alike.

Women volunteer leaders and board members are the ones who inspire us to accomplish much for our organizations. Only through this powerful coalition will we, as female development officers, not only break through the glass ceiling but gain the satisfaction of being able to perform true service.

The partnership model of development and the emerging role of women in philanthropy will bring increased financial support and true change for the better for our institutions—and ultimately a better life for our children. Let us partner with philanthropists—women and men—to further altruistic philanthropy, advance the common good, and ensure a bright future for *all* our world's children.

References

Addams, J. *Twenty Years at Hull House*. Signet: New York, 1910.

Blair, K. H. *Torchbearers*. Bloomington: Indiana University Press, 1994.

Blum, D. *Sex on the Brain: The Biological Differences Between Men and Women*. New York: Viking, 1997.

Kuczmanski, S. S., and Kuczmanski, T. *Values-Based Leadership*. Englewood Cliffs, N.J.: Prentice Hall, 1995.

Ostrower, F. *Why the Wealthy Give: The Culture of Elite Philanthropy*. Princeton, N.J.: Princeton University Press, 1995.

Pyne, A., and Robertson, D. "Charities Marketing—More Focus on the Beneficiary," *Journal of Nonprofit and Voluntary Sector Marketing*, 1997, 2 (2).

Rosso, H. *Rosso on Fund Raising: Lessons from a Master's Lifetime Experience*. San Francisco: Jossey-Bass, 1996.

Shaw, S., and Taylor, M. *Reinventing Fundraising: Realizing the Potential of Women's Philanthropy.* San Francisco: Jossey-Bass, 1995.

Turner, R. C. "Metaphors Fund Raisers Live By: Language and Reality in Fund Raising." In D. F. Burlingame and L. J. Hulse (eds.), *Taking Fund Raising Seriously: Advancing the Profession and Practice of Raising Money.* San Francisco: Jossey-Bass, 1991.

Wuthnow, R., and Hodgkinson, V. *Faith and Philanthropy in America: Exploring the Role of Religion in America's Voluntary Sector.* San Francisco: Jossey-Bass, 1990.

MARTHA A. TAYLOR *is vice president of the University of Wisconsin Foundation and is coauthor, with Sondra Shaw, of* Reinventing Fundraising: Realizing the Potential of Women's Philanthropy.

Women have been an important part of the national philanthropy movement, and as pathfinders they are providing new leadership styles at the highest levels of fundraising management.

2

Executive women in development: Career paths, life choices, and advancing to the top

Sondra Shaw-Hardy

WHAT DOES IT TAKE to be the fundraising CEO of a large organization or institution? Are there differences in the ways men and women move ahead in the development profession? Is being a woman an advantage or a disadvantage?

During the last decade as I moved up the ladder from running a two-person shop to a sixteen-person office, I occasionally pondered these questions. All the while, I observed that men in fundraising continued to dominate the top management positions and typically were paid higher salaries than women. Fortunately, as increasing numbers of women continue to enter the development profession, more are ready to move into positions of top leadership as CEOs and directors of development.

This chapter describes the fundraising backgrounds and values of a select group of women fundraising executives, what they bring to their job, the things that have motivated and troubled them as women, and what may lie ahead for them personally and for their

NEW DIRECTIONS FOR PHILANTHROPIC FUNDRAISING, NO. 19, SPRING 1998 © JOSSEY-BASS PUBLISHERS

profession. I have spoken to a number of women at various meetings and conferences over the last two years and have included their observations in this chapter. In addition, I interviewed five prominent women in fundraising management. The women interviewed were Marion Brown, a vice president at the University of Wisconsin Foundation; Patricia Lewis, former president and CEO of the National Society of Fund Raising Executives; Nancy Loshkajian, executive director of development, University Advancement, University of California, Santa Cruz; Doretha Mortimore, senior vice president for development, Indiana University Foundation (before that, she was associate vice president for development at Michigan State University); and Karen Stone, director for development, University of New Mexico, and president of the University of New Mexico Foundation.

These extraordinary and successful women reflect many similar values and background experiences, and they were delighted to share their thoughts. They are extremely knowledgeable about their profession and believe that what they are doing is making a strong contribution to a better society.

The average salary of the women interviewed is $105,000 per year, and they are (or were) responsible for raising anywhere from $8.2 to $110 million annually. They supervise ten to thirty-five full-time employees and control budgets ranging from $2 to $6 million. Their educational backgrounds include an M.B.A., Ed.D., M.M., M.F.A., and a B.S. in business and marketing. They have been in their current or most recent positions from one to seven years. Together, they have eighty-four years of fundraising experience.

Entering the fundraising field

When the interviewees began their fundraising careers, there were not many colleges or universities teaching development or philanthropy as a profession. Thus, most of them came to the field primarily through volunteer work. Karen Stone cut her teeth on fundraising for political candidates. Her first job was as a political

aide for the Los Angeles city attorney. Because of her high visibility, she caught the eye of her alma mater, the University of
Chicago, and they recruited her to head up fundraising for their
western regional office.

Patricia Lewis said that volunteer work was a real key to her first
job in fundraising. She had served on a number of boards and as a
volunteer fundraiser had written grant proposals and prepared
printed materials and brochures. Never shy about asking for help or
networking, Lewis visited a friend in a public relations firm who
reviewed her eclectic background and advised her to go into the nonprofit area. Lewis ended up creating a fundraising position for herself in a major organization. She said that may not happen as much
now as it did twenty years ago because today's organizations better
understand the need for fundraisers and already have them on board.

Some of the women felt it was helpful to begin working in a
smaller organization so as to learn every aspect of fundraising.
Lewis said, "I think it's very important for anyone entering this field
to get a good grounding in fundraising, including the annual fund
as well as planned giving. In a small organization you have to wear
many hats, sometimes even marketing and public relations, which
can help strengthen your career choices. Once you know things
from a generalist point of view, then you can decide whether to spe-
cialize or go into management. At that time, it is important to pick
an educational track and learn all you can about the specialized area
and become the best possible fundraiser or manager in the area of
your choice."

Nancy Loshkajian initially pursued an opera career and then got
her first major fundraising job at Indiana University after obtaining
a master's degree there. She said, "I was the development officer for
the dean of students, which meant mostly annual gifts. This was not
an easy area to raise money for, but it gave me an opportunity to run
my own shop with a secretary, as small as it might have been."

Lewis said life is often serendipity. "I believe that one can strate-
gize for long-range direction, but you can't plan all the steps. If
you keep yourself open to opportunities you never know what will
happen."

Doretha Mortimore entered the field from a faculty and administrative position at Western Michigan University. She wanted to stay in academia but also have connections to what she calls "the real world," so she answered an ad for an assistant director of the annual fund at the university. She credits her work experience in the membership area with her hometown chamber of commerce as giving her the necessary background to believe she could do the job.

Academia was also the route for Marion Brown. She was on the faculty in the School of Human Ecology at the University of Wisconsin-Madison. A colleague told her about a fundraising position at the UW Foundation. Brown said she did not know much about fundraising other than through her work as a volunteer, but she had responsibility for an outreach program and thought that those skills matched the position. In addition, she recognized that her faculty experience and knowledge of the university could be a strong asset.

In each case the women became aware of an opportunity, and even though they might not have had all the skills necessary for the job, they were not afraid to try. They did not lock themselves into what they were doing but rather looked at their past experience and asked how it might fit into the new job. As they moved ahead in their careers, they were bold enough to use the advantages of their positions and background to help drive them.

Expertise that matters

What does it take to become a fundraiser? Are there any particular skills and personality traits that help? Mortimore said, "There are many personal qualities and skills required for success. However, among the top are excellent verbal and written communication skills, plus the maturity necessary to deal with the politics of most university environments. Skills in negotiation and compromise are also important."

Lewis thought that knowing financial management is "terribly important." She said, "Too often women do not have the financial background necessary for important jobs in today's market." She points out how essential it is to continue learning because things in the financial area are always changing. Stone said she understood the need for training in finance, and that was the reason she obtained her M.B.A. This degree has provided her with the skills she felt were necessary to head up her university's foundation, including being a part of the investment and asset allocation processes.

Loshkajian said, "I knew nothing about finance and certainly wish I had." However, education played an important part in Loshkajian's success. She credits Hank Rosso's fundraising school and CASE (Council for the Advancement and Support of Education) conferences with giving her the tools she needed to continue moving into more responsible positions.

Knowing how to negotiate was something most felt was of the utmost importance. Lewis thought many women were intimidated by this and that many seemed afraid to take risks. "The first time I advocated for a particular salary I was scared to death," she said. "I didn't have another offer; one seldom does when negotiating for a new job, and I would have had to start all over if they hadn't accepted my bottom line." She said an NSFRE study showed that people wanted training in negotiation skills, and consequently this is now a part of NSFRE's conference class schedules. Lewis pointed out that their classes are not only for women but for men who, as they get older, can also become fearful about salary negotiations.

Stone said that because of the different socialization that occurs when they are young, boys often learn more negotiation skills than girls. "We were trained not to be pushy. But I've learned if you don't ask, you're not going to be rewarded. That is certainly true in the fundraising area. In negotiating for my last job, I used my network and called other women to find out what they asked for and what I was missing. I called another colleague in executive recruitment and picked her brain about retirement issues."

As for salary negotiations, they found it is much easier to ask for and get that additional five or ten thousand dollars up front rather than after they had taken the job. Most nonprofits give modest percentage salary increases each year, and it is virtually impossible to get that kind of money through such small incremental raises. This proved especially true for Mortimore, who said, "If I hadn't learned to negotiate, my last two salaries would have been woefully below my male counterparts'."

A passion for the job

All of the women felt that to be successful they had to have a passion about what they were doing. Loshkajian had no formal training in fundraising. She did, however, have a passion for the arts that she credits with obtaining her job at the University of Cincinnati Conservatory of Music. She said, "The donor knows and can sense whether you really care about what you're raising money for." Mortimore believes that giving money is an empowering action and said, "Passion for a cause is essential in fundraising. If you're not committed and invested yourself, how can you expect to empower others?"

But how does this passion translate into action? After passion for the cause has been expressed, should sales or marketing be used to persuade people to give? The women most emphatically felt that there were significant differences between selling and philanthropy. Loshkajian said, "We don't sell products. We may market and promote the institution and use some similar techniques. But the difference is the donor doesn't have to give us a gift. They give from their heart. Something in their humanity makes them do this, and they want to give to someone who cares about the institution."

Working with and for women

Several of the interviewees experienced some professional disappointments because of the way other women treated them. Whether it is from jealousy or not understanding the fundamentals of teamwork, women can sometimes be their own worst enemies.

Lewis said, "I have not always found women to be as supportive as I would have expected and that was terribly disappointing. But sometimes I think I may look for things in a woman that I wouldn't look for in a man and have to watch myself to make sure that doesn't happen. If I were to make a gross generalization, I would say that women have a harder time letting go of feelings and going on with life. I think this will change as more young girls participate in team sports, because you have to let it go if the pitcher doesn't pitch well or the catcher doesn't catch the ball. You realize they made a mistake and just go on with it. Unfortunately, we don't have a real grounding in this yet."

Stone explained, "I have had some profound disappointments, but this is not an overwhelming observation. There can be incredible pettiness among some female staff that is very frustrating to deal with. They don't always see the big picture, and it's a challenge to help them feel they are part of the team. Sometimes it's because they have been thrust into high-level positions and don't have the necessary self-confidence to deal with this and they're scared. As a consequence, they perceive setting goals and objectives and being held accountable as very threatening. I have learned that bringing in new, experienced staff to serve as role models and mentor these women, often on the QT, has been very helpful."

Fortunately, there are many documented cases of women supporting and helping each other succeed. The women interviewed for this chapter are strong examples of this philosophy. Often the women who are most problematic are not those who head up organizations. The difficulty often lies with the women peers on staff—women in the organization with whom you must work.

On working for women, Lewis said, "This can be a power issue and power issues are important. I have asked people when they were interviewing whether they would have a problem working for a woman. No one ever got angry at the question. They explained to me how they had worked with women and almost every single time there was no problem." That has been my experience too. In fact, I have had many staffers say they preferred me as a boss because I took the time to work with them and they could sense my interest in them personally.

The other side of the issue was, is it more difficult managing men or women? Lewis thought that supervising men can be easier because men seem to retain some child-like traits their whole lives and like the sense of mothering and nurturing they get from a woman. She also said, "I feel men are more free to be honest and thus it's easier to get along with them because you know where they stand. This goes back to women still feeling they have to prove themselves. Men have disagreements and then it's over with."

The view from the top

There is an incredible difference between being a staff member in an office and being in charge of the office. It is nearly impossible to be really good friends with your employees, and it can also be dangerous. Sharing confidences can be risky, particularly if relationships change. It is also much harder to give a poor performance review, or to discipline or fire someone who is your friend. Loshkajian said, "At this level, you can't have friends who work directly for you. It's difficult to set professional expectations and then be the friend who has to hold them accountable to meet those expectations." Women frequently want to bond with others—male and female—but as bosses, that bonding must be professional, not personal.

Stone said, "I am very aware that you cannot be best friends with everybody. Nor should you be. That is not your goal. You're there to do a job, do it well, and help everybody else do well. I knew this when I made the shift from running a regional office to working for a major research university. It was a revelation that with greater management responsibility came an awareness that I was a role model. I had to consciously be thinking what that meant and what I wanted to communicate to my staff and colleagues. Nobody told me. It just came with the territory."

Most found friends in other organizations or elsewhere inside their own to confide in, discuss our problems with, and even laugh with about management frustrations. But to a person they agreed this has to happen externally—outside the office. The truth of the matter is that the challenge and excitement that comes from being in charge has to take the place of the warm, amiable office friendships that occurred as staffers.

According to Brown, people are not as open with those at the top. She said, "It's harder to get information the higher up you go. People are much more careful about what they say to you and less willing to share because they're not sure of the impact it will have on them." Brown also feels a greater sense of overall responsibility for the organization and the people she is managing than she did as a staff person. "It's different now because I want success for the entire organization. I look at the organization in a different way because there's more to consider. As a staffer I worked on behalf of my constituency. Now I see things in the whole and my perspective has changed. I have to take more things into consideration about what works, not only for a particular unit but for the development office and the total university."

Mortimore said that it is lonely at the top but if you keep focused on the highest quality in terms of results and process, it is greatly satisfying. "My most enjoyable moments have been those in which I knew I had empowered people—employees and donors! I love planning and executing and helping others to do likewise. However, at the top be prepared for all kinds of nastiness." Mortimore said that the role politics plays in academic fundraising was more than she could have imagined. "Power struggles are common and men are constantly attempting to expand or defend their turf. Some women do too but it's more prevalent with men." She thinks men do this because they may be threatened by women in positions of power and authority and that these power issues can make it very difficult to do an excellent job.

As top administrators and managers, Lewis, Loshkajian, and Brown were all surprised to find out how much time they spent recruiting and managing staff. Lewis said, "Hiring, nurturing, training, and matching people with jobs is very challenging and exceedingly time consuming. I find it is also draining emotionally. On the other hand, if it works, it's one of the most rewarding parts of the job." Brown said that she has less time to work with donors because "management takes a lot of time if you're going to bring in and foster the development of good people."

Loshkajian shared Brown's desire to spend more time raising money. She said, "I would like to do more fundraising, but it's hard to make time to do this and manage staff, deal with budgets, and develop plans. I find I can now only spend about 10 to 15 percent of my time in direct contact with donors, and I miss not having more of that." Loshkajian hopes now that she has the organization and infrastructure in place, she can get out more to visit with donors.

Management style and philosophy

The author of *In Search of Excellence*, Tom Peters (1997), said that the results of a two-year study by Lawrence A. Pfaff and Associates show that women outscored men in fifteen of twenty managerial categories. These included the hard categories such as "planning," "goal setting," and "decisiveness."

In discussing their management style, the major thrust for the interviewees seemed to be creating the right kind of atmosphere for staff to do their very best. Lewis said, "I believe in a flat rather than a hierarchical organization with a very small group making the ultimate decisions. But input into these decisions should come from the departments and everyone should feel a part of the process. However, this is sometimes hard to do because not every department head on the team finds it comfortable to include others in their decision making."

Stone too felt it important to have staff input into decision making and has formed a senior management team that advises her weekly. But she pointed out that she seeks outside advice too and makes an effort to go out of her way to listen to what the academic community is saying. She also believes in encouraging and recognizing her staff's accomplishments and does this through a development newsletter that gets sent to the entire university community. She said, "In it, I have a column where I recognize my staff, and they see the newsletter and what I have said about them." She thinks it is important in daily activities and meetings to never forget that "we have an ongoing management responsibility to people, and it has to always be there in the front brain lobe. I try to communicate that to staff and advocate for them. I also try to be a good listener, even when the message is critical. I try not to forget what it was like to have been out there as a staff person."

Lewis agreed about encouraging staff. She said, "As a CEO, I find it extremely rewarding when my staff does something remarkable. I had someone who recently achieved a Ph.D. after fifteen years and I couldn't have been prouder. I see this as a nurturing thing and wonder if some of the rewards I get are because of my need to nurture. Perhaps a way to characterize my management style would be to call it benevolent matriarchy premised on a strong management team."

Mortimore described her management philosophy as empowering people and leading by example. "My style is extremely team-oriented—which many times drives power people crazy! I have never shied away from where I know the buck stops, meaning, I will make the decisions, but I also believe the best ones come with optimal input and involvement by the whole team. Consensus building is the best route." Stone agreed but added, "I used to describe myself as a consensus manager and by and large that is true. But there are moments that you're alone and you hope that you've done a good job collecting critical information needed in making a decision."

Brown believes in the team approach as well as giving staff the tools needed to do their job. To her this means providing more guidance and assistance when staff first come on board and backup when it is needed. Additionally, she mentioned that one of the major challenges managers have is realizing that not all people are alike. "We need to foster the growth of the person who doesn't quite fit the same mold as everyone else. The challenge is to retain the person's individuality while making things work for the good of the organization," she said.

Some of the women were concerned about working with the fundraising goals they themselves have to meet versus setting realistic goals and expectations for staff. Loshkajian said, "Even though this is a bottom-line business, it is very important to set realistic goals and expectations for staff. I try not to set unrealistic goals based primarily on what the administration's budget needs are. There must be enough prospects for staff to carry out that goal and resources to get the job done." Stone agreed with her. "I am a strong advocate for staff and getting what they need to do their job well. They are our major resource and we must help them do the best job they can."

Stone goes so far as to occasionally set goals that may mean her staff will leave. She said, "I am proactive in helping provide staff encouragement to establish personal goals for themselves in their careers and openly discuss where they would like to be. If it is not in my organization, that's OK because I believe in helping them better themselves so they can move on."

The women were not afraid to let their staff make mistakes as long as they learned from them. Loshkajian said, "I try to pay attention to my staff and manage in a way that speaks to where they need encouragement or prodding. When they do well, I encourage them. If they don't do well, I ask them to learn from the experience and be as clear as possible about what they would do the next time. The important thing to me is the willingness on the part of an employee to try hard."

Lewis admitted this is an admirable goal but said, "Often the organization's bottom line enters into the process. Part of my nature is not to expect anyone to do what I wouldn't do myself. This may be a female trait, I'm not sure. But I do know that I'm very demanding of myself and others. I expect everyone to do it right. Even though I may not technically be responsible for the actions of everyone in the organization, ultimately I am and this can occasionally cause me to be defensive when someone makes a mistake, for I take personal responsibility for all that goes on. I am very loyal to staff and tell them it's all right to make mistakes and then move on. But sometimes outcome and accountability bring this up short. My style is inclusive but not as much as I would always like because of pressure and the bottom line."

The women agreed that being an administrator sometimes required disciplining or letting staff go and this is never easy. Lewis said, "When mistakes are made, I try to help my staff see how to approach things the next time and am very forgiving, but at some point I have to say no more. Asking someone to leave is never easy, but the organization must come first. I try to do this with dignity and look at it as a mismatch rather than a failure."

Although only two of the women entered the workforce with small children to care for, most were familiar with the issues. Lewis had this to say about management and child care: "I remember being torn by guilt when I had small children and was working full-time. So I know how important it is to work in an environment where there's a reasonable amount of flexibility allowed for child care for both women and men. One of my management staff works full-time for four rather than five days a week. She tries hard to make sure everyone knows she is putting in more than forty hours a week. This is a two-way street, because she works over and above what she might do otherwise since she appreciates my concern for her child care needs." Lewis does not just do this for women. She supports her male management staff by giving them the same kind of child care flexibility and urges them to do the same for their staff.

Loshkajian offered these last few tips on management along with a reminder to herself. "The thing I've learned about management in the last few years is that everyone is different. I have to adapt my style to their needs. What motivates one may be different for someone else so I have to be a coach and be flexible. But what I probably don't do enough of is encouragement. I'm more prodding and perhaps need to work on being more encouraging and supportive."

Staff issues and institutional support

Good management requires making good decisions about hiring. I asked Brown what she looks for when she interviews people. She said she takes into account the way a person communicates and the transferable skill experience the candidate has that can apply to the position. The ability to listen and not go on and on about themselves is also on her list, as is the ability to make others feel comfortable. She wants a high level of energy and a sense from candidates that they want and can do the job, which in this case means representing the university well. Finally, she seeks candidates who can handle multiple tasks simultaneously while paying attention to detail. "I need to know if they can answer three phone calls in a row about different projects while dictating a letter to a donor and signing their name on two other letters at the same time. This too is what being a good fundraiser is all about," she said.

Volunteering is important to Brown because she is a volunteer and looks for an aspirant who has worked with volunteers and also gives their own time to nonprofits. Someone who is too aggressive or bottom-line oriented concerns Brown, who said, "If the candidate is too sales minded then this probably isn't the right place for her. While it's true we're interested in raising funds, we stress the importance of developing long-term relationships between the university and our friends."

Brown went on to explain how important relationship-building skills are. "Those relationships will ultimately lead to support. We're not out there just chatting or being friendly, nor are we simply selling a product. We want to give people opportunities to invest in our institution. The more they understand how the university is addressing their concerns, the more likely they are to be involved. There is a great deal of competition for the philanthropic dollar and people are making increasingly thoughtful decisions about their gifts. They're looking at their priorities and if the university shows it is addressing those priorities, they will support us."

Compensation

One issue that brought an immediate response from women is compensation. Most had been in jobs where they made less than their male counterparts and had to work hard to ensure that it did not happen again. Mortimore's career has spanned eighteen years, and she succinctly explained the issue by saying, "Only in my last two jobs was my compensation equal to or greater than my male counterparts."

Not receiving commensurate pay to men is something the women found very demeaning. Stone said, "In my first development position my compensation level was not equal to that of the male I replaced. Because I didn't have all the experience he had, I believed I just needed to prove myself. But my compensation was never adjusted to my satisfaction based on my performance, so I made a decision that I was in a negative situation and needed to move on."

Loshkajian recalled that early in her career this was a heavily male-dominated profession and, even at public institutions, her male colleagues made more than she did. She believes the equity issue is still very prevalent, although she thinks we are at the leading edge of change in that regard. But she said, "I still see men brought in as associate and assistant vice presidents at higher salaries than women would receive. A woman has to really negotiate well for herself."

Although Lewis found she was making less than her predecessor in one of her earlier jobs, she was fortunate to have two women board members come to her aid. They presented a good case, and shortly thereafter she received the compensation that put her in the same category as her predecessors. She found support again when a woman board member of another nonprofit she was working for, whom she described as a "real fighter," found out she was being paid less than males in similar jobs in the community. The woman took on the issue and Lewis's salary was increased. She said, "I fought hard for equal compensation because I thought it was so important to be perceived as an equal."

Conversely, some women volunteers do not believe a woman deserves to be paid adequately for a job they consider to be something a volunteer could do, such as fundraising. The interesting part is that they often feel a man should be paid handsomely for that same job, just because he is a man. To compound things, if the women are wealthy they may never have had an outside job nor understand what is necessary to make ends meet. This gives them very little comprehension of the financial realities of life. Margaret A. Duronio and Eugene R. Tempel discuss moving from volunteer to paid staff in their book *Fund Raisers* (1997). "Women must take responsibility for becoming more knowledgeable about competitive salaries and about what they should expect to earn based on experience, education, geographic region, and type of organization. They must be cautious of exploitation when moving from volunteer to paid positions and from part-time to full-time status" (p. 185).

Lewis pointed out what sometimes happens when volunteers move into fairly significant positions in the nonprofit workforce. She said, "If their husbands have good positions, they may not need additional household income, or they may be willing to accept less compensation because they know the organization doesn't have much money. And of course, when they were volunteering they received no pay, so even a little is more than nothing. I recall a woman who had been in the business sector and moved into the nonprofit as a CEO at half the salary because she considered that to be her contribution. We all worked on her to get her salary up because she was not bringing a sense of esteem to her position or anyone else's. She did this over time, but it was very hard for her, although her own low compensation kept all salaries in her organization lower. She was even willing to pay those who worked for her more than she got. I realize this was her personal decision but not necessarily a good one for the profession and particularly for women."

Obstacles facing women in development

Power, credibility, lack of women's support for one another, and women finding an icebreaker common language with men were issues that some of the women talked about having to deal with as they moved into administrative and management positions. Mortimore said, "The major obstacle I have faced is being a woman in a position of power and authority. Strong women threaten some men. Also we still live in a society where many older men and women cannot fathom professional, working women. I have had experiences—thankfully infrequently—where prospects or donors have asked if I was a secretary to the male dean or administrator I was staffing."

Stone talked about the difference in people's perceptions of credibility between women and men but said the credibility issue ultimately had helped her become stronger. "There is still a dismissive attitude in some sectors when a woman shows up. Sometimes she doesn't have as much credibility as a man would. I don't believe this impeded my career, but I must admit I have gotten bristly at times when I felt people were discounting me because of my gender. But this only served to inspire me to further my education and get what I perceived to be the necessary credentials—an M.B.A."

Lewis agreed with the credibility issue and said, "Sometimes I felt I was not taken seriously. I believe males are frequently regarded more seriously than women just because they're males. There were also times when those who did take me seriously had extremely high expectations. The reality is that women have to work harder than men to prove their validity and be taken seriously." She offered the suggestion that women could gain greater respect from others by helping one another. "Maybe women need to support one another more and not expect perfection from each other. There are some astounding women out there but how frequently do we see women express accolades for one another? I know some remarkable women but there isn't a sense of collaborative energy for them."

Women and men's icebreakers or conversation openers was a topic of interest to Brown. "Men have a common language and that's sports. Finding that starting point can be a challenge for women," she said. Brown has worked in the corporate-foundation area and said she thinks men representing companies are more accustomed to having women in the workplace. Consequently, they often find it easier talking with women about corporate gifts than male donors do in talking about their individual gifts. But she also feels that once men get past the initial uneasiness in talking with a woman, they may become more conversant because they feel they can be more open with a woman. An interesting aspect Brown brought up was that sometimes women's voices are not heard as well as men's. She said, "I've been in meetings and said something that, when a man repeated it, was better received. I don't think it's because men's voices are louder; I just think they are sometimes taken more seriously by other men. But I am hopeful that as more women enter into management positions and as we see and, more importantly, hear more women on the radio and television, men will become better able to hear what women are saying."

Career moves and evaluating opportunities

Statistics show that men and women in development careers average about three years before moving on to their next job, which can be a higher position within the same organization. Most of our interviewees fit that pattern, with their time on the job ranging from one to ten years in a total of twenty-seven jobs. This has provided them not only with experience in negotiating salaries as described earlier but also in interviewing for new jobs. They were well aware of the pitfalls involved in changing jobs and the questions that need to be asked before accepting the next position. The truth is, though, that we do not always ask those questions or really examine that new job. This can be because we are anxious to get out of a bad situation or want to move into something with more responsibility or a higher salary.

Loshkajian agreed and added that it is important to avoid taking on jobs that are not achievable. "We need to be smart about the jobs we choose because if there are a lot of unrealistic expectations we are doomed to fail. We should look at the resources, commitment from the CEO including their time, and if the institution has a strategic plan or the willingness to adopt one," she said.

The women felt it was of the utmost importance to know all the facts about a potential new job before taking it and to know exactly to whom they would be reporting. The top fundraiser in the organization should report directly to the president or CEO. Chances are they will be briefing and even critiquing the CEO. Having this responsibility requires the authoritative and titular position to go with it. Unfortunately, if the president is a male he may still regard women as secretaries or assistants. However, most people are influenced by titles and will listen much better to someone with the title of vice president for institutional advancement than to a director of development who reports to someone else.

Along that same line, the top development person must be president of the organization's foundation, should there be one. This position generally deals with the board charged with raising money for the organization. These volunteers are chosen for their ability to give and get, and they need to regard the top fundraiser (not someone else in the organization) as being their leader. Stone said, "I believe my credibility is greater with the academic community and with external constituencies because I am president of our foundation as well as director of development."

Benefits of being a woman in development

Are women better fundraisers than men and, if so, what skills and attitudes do they have that help them? Do these same abilities affect not only donors and prospects but volunteers and boards also? I asked the interviewees about this and most felt that women do have special skills that have helped them in their careers. They named these as listening, nurturing, being open, being empathetic, building relationships, and attending to detail.

Loshkajian talked about listening and said, "I believe women are better fundraisers than men because we listen better. Women are more sensitive in our interpretation of what we hear and more open minded to listening to what a donor wants." She attributed this to women's socialization and expectations that they will listen to and be aware of people.

Mortimore believed that philanthropy and fundraising are fortunate to have women in development because generally women are better at being empathetic than men. But she was hopeful this will change as male-female and mother-son relationships develop. Relationship building ranked high on Lewis, Brown, and Stone's lists. Lewis said, "I think women are pretty much into relationship building and nurturing and that's the greatest strength in being a woman." She also feels women "are perfectionists and into detail work, which is absolutely essential in fundraising."

Stone said, "I think that I have, as a woman, more fine-tuned antennae to listen well and read body language. I think other strong assets are my relationship-building skills. I feel I am tuned into people's emotional side and know that appearances don't always reflect what's going on inside. These same skills are reflected in how we manage and deal with boards, business, and political leaders." Stone particularly identifies political leaders because she said they are the ones who determine much of the fate of our major research universities.

Not all of the interviewees felt as strongly that women have characteristics that make them better fundraisers. Brown said, "It might just be my experience but I think the differences between men and women aren't as glaring as people sometimes think they are. I have found that men who are good in this profession know how to listen too."

Words of wisdom for success

Not surprisingly, the women had many, many words of wisdom about what they felt had contributed to their success. In fact, Mortimore thought there were as many different ways to succeed as there are types of people. But what is most important, she said, is, "Women should focus on the job, work hard, and look for opportunities."

Mortimore suggested being well aware of what moving into a top management position means and offered some suggestions for survival. She cautioned about the importance of carefully considering how far you really want to go in management by saying, "Sometimes women—as well as men—keep moving up the ladder and don't take time to do a serious cost-benefit analysis. Consider carefully what you enjoy most about the profession, and if bringing in gifts is your greatest joy, don't believe you must be promoted into top-level management positions just to be considered a success. I also encourage women to befriend and help female colleagues; don't consider them competition." She concluded with some practical and inspirational advice: "Watch out for burnout, overcommitting, and expecting perfection of yourself. And avoid thinking you can't do what you want to do."

Working in the major gift area is the way to success, according to Loshkajian. "If you want to be seen as a successful fundraiser and move up in an organization, you have to have as much contact as possible with donors. And the way to do that is to be in major gifts. Then you can take up management. But to get there you have to be able to raise money, talk to donors, ask for and get the gift. If you can do that, you're valuable to an organization and will be noticed and presented with management opportunities."

When you are busy and successful, it is not always easy to take care of your health. Stone's words of wisdom involved taking care of yourself. She said, "Exercise is very important in keeping my sanity. I started taking yoga and getting massages more often, and I may even take up golf."

Asked for her words of wisdom, Brown said, "For women the opportunities are there and it's a matter of taking advantage of them. We should look for opportunities, find the gaps or needs, and be willing to fill those needs. Every job that needs to be done doesn't have a job description." She agreed with Stone about the reasons for exercising and pointed out that the health club provides women with opportunities men have always had in doing business. "I saw a faculty member at a gym and asked her a question about a meeting she attended recently. She said she loved it because now women are having these conversations in locker rooms as men have for years. I see this as a reflection of our changing times for women where interacting in an informal setting can have as much to do with your success as in a formal one."

Other pieces of advice from Brown were: "Don't whine and adopt a 'poor me' or victim attitude; be willing to take credit for things; don't be afraid of management, as most men don't know any more about it than women; don't think you have to be perfect, just prepared; continuously study your profession and how to do it better; take every opportunity you can to speak or chair program committees; and practice, practice your presentations in front of a mirror and out loud."

How gender is changing fundraising

With women making up more than 50 percent of the development positions (Duronio and Tempel, 1997), the interviewees had some very interesting and perhaps unexpected responses to the subject. Two of them worried that the profession might be getting out of balance, and one was wary of the pendulum swinging back.

Although Loshkajian's staff is primarily women, she said she does not recruit with that in mind and hopes we do not end up with too many women in the profession. She was thinking about her prospects and donors and the best person to work with them when she said, "We should have a balanced approach because we need people with different sensitivities to relate to each of our donors. I would really like to see more talented men come into the profession. My feelings have less to do with compensation and the whole feminization of the profession and more to do with finding the best people to deal with our donors and prospects."

Lewis said she has seen increasing numbers of women come into the field and was looking forward to the day when they held more of the better jobs. She agreed that the profession should not get too out of balance and thought compensation was a potential problem. She said, "I have a concern that the profession not become too gender-oriented either way so we can better balance salary and compensation levels and opportunities. There has been an uncomfortable history in other fields when a predominantly male field became primarily female. This resulted in a loss of compensation, although I'm not sure that would happen now because women are speaking out more."

Stone too was anxious that women move up in the profession but cautioned about losing ground. She said, "I'm acutely aware that progress can be lost very quickly. When I came to UNM, three of the top positions on campus were [filled by] women and they're all gone now."

Personal satisfaction in a fundraising career

Listening to the interviewees describe the personal satisfaction they receive from their careers, one can surely understand why they are so successful. The genuine interest they have in their donors has to be a major reason for their outstanding accomplishments as professional fundraisers. Loshkajian spoke for most of them when she said, "The important part of my life is to have worked directly with donors and helped them accomplish something they really wanted to make happen."

Seeing donors become empowered brought joy to Stone. She said, "Working with donors has provided me with the greatest personal satisfaction. It's about empowerment—helping them feel they really made a good decision about their giving, wherever it ends up on campus. There's an intrinsic, almost spiritual side to this that you can't begin to put a price on."

Lewis said her satisfaction is three-fold: "first, seeing the results of the use of contributed money. It is so satisfactory to see programs develop and the way they impact people's lives—to know that I have helped people through the work I've done. The second is experiencing the pleasure that donors have when they feel their contribution is making a difference. Getting a check is not nearly as satisfactory to me as a follow-up visit when I tell the donor what we did with the check and then see the glow in the donor's face. And third is knowing that something you worked hard on for long periods of time really does come to a fruitful conclusion where the donor, organization, and beneficiary feel good."

But let's also not forget the fun part of the job. Loshkajian pointed out that she had had the chance to meet people she never would have been able to meet otherwise—CEOs in their private dining rooms, for example.

Mortimore and Brown conveyed the sense of joy the interviewees felt about what they do. Mortimore said, "Aren't we lucky to be in such a great profession! There are days when we see certain things that make us despair, but overall it's great!" Brown agreed, saying that fundraising is a wonderful career and "I consider myself very fortunate to be in this profession. I believe in higher education's ability to solve problems, and I have the opportunity to meet caring people who have the means and interest to help us solve those problems. So I feel very lucky to be able to mesh the two together."

Women and philanthropy

The women interviewed have been an important part of the national women and philanthropy movement. They have all been extremely supportive and in some cases have broken new ground themselves. We credit their efforts and the efforts of others throughout the country with the fact that between 1994 and 1997, and for the first time in history, women's giving from their annual income was greater than men's (Gray, 1996). Although work with women and philanthropy began as early as 1988, it was during the three years from 1994 to 1997 that a concentration of education, programming, and media attention was especially focused on this subject. Even more important, during those same three years the research showed that women's average contribution increased by 26 percent, while men's increased only 6 percent.

Each of the women interviewed had either a direct role or definite interest in the subject, and I asked them both to share their thoughts about the topic and a favorite personal example of women's giving.

Mortimore observed, "In the several instances where I have dealt personally with women as major donors, they had to be devoted to the subject or cause and very involved. Some men as major donors are like this, but I believe women invest differently and must be approached differently. None of these women 'controlled' their finances, but they knew the assets were theirs as well as their husbands' and felt empowered enough to make six- and seven-figure gifts. They also told their husbands they were going to do it."

According to Loshkajian, "Women are becoming more conscious and confident of their ability to make philanthropic decisions. In general, I believe they are emerging from behind the shadows and into the forefront. As that emergence continues, women will use their resources to make a difference and a change. One story that means a lot to me demonstrates how making a long-term investment in working with women can pay off. When I was at Cincinnati I worked very closely with a woman who headed the alumni board. She was a donor at the university and gave $1,000 a year. For some people that might not have been a lot, but she was a working mom and for her it was. When we got into the capital campaign, she wanted to see to it that alumni giving was equal to or larger than the amount the institution's community friends gave. We worked very closely together and I knew she wanted to do something meaningful. Two years after I left, she took the time to call me at Santa Cruz to tell me that she had made an important decision. Because of the work I did with her, she had decided to pledge $25,000 to the capital campaign. She said by my working with her and others, I helped her take a position of leadership and set the pace for the alumni board. It was very gratifying to me that the seeds I had planted and cultivated were important enough for her to make her decision and that she called me personally to tell me. She really appreciated the impact I had had there. Going from giving $1,000 a year to $5,000 a year demonstrated a lot of growth for her as a woman. My guess is she will continue to work to ensure that other alumni and women follow her example."

The growth of women's participation in couple giving has provided Brown with a great deal of satisfaction. She said, "I was pleased when I started out with a male donor and his wife became involved. She understood the importance of the project and supported it as well. There is a woman I'm working with now who is a donor and will give more over time. Her husband has been active on university boards and committees for years. I am delighted to say she is now serving on a board, is a volunteer leader for a project, and has made a gift. She's at the point of making her own decisions about university projects but still tells me to call her husband when I bring up money. She is beginning to understand that it's their money because their relationship is a partnership."

Stone proudly explained, "One of most important things I've ever done is the research with women philanthropists and establishing a permanent program at UCLA. This program has become vibrant and strong and a role model for the rest of country. Being involved as a facilitator in helping to heighten the awareness of the importance of women and their ability to make a difference with their philanthropy has been the most profound contribution I have made in the field of development. I incorporate it in everything I do in my profession." Lewis had a wonderful example: "I have a friend who is a classic illustration of what is happening. She has significant means and has, over the last ten years, really begun to educate herself about how she wants to use that money for the better good. It's been great fun watching her experience and growth. First of all she wanted to respond to every little request but realized she did not get a whole lot of feeling of accomplishment doing that. Now she supports six to eight nonprofits. But I know she will continue to evolve. I sense that the next thing that's coming is a large gift to a specific program. I can see that happening in the not-too-far-off future. This is an illustration of what is happening because we are paying attention to women as donors. They are getting the kind of attention they didn't used to get. We are now seeing women who feel they have more control over their finances than they previously had. This is new. These women want to know they have a sense of control in their finances and their philanthropy."

References

Duronio, M., and Tempel, E. *Fund Raisers.* San Francisco: Jossey-Bass, 1997.
Gray, S. "Charities See Bigger Gifts, Fewer Givers." *Chronicle of Philanthropy,* Oct. 17, 1996, p. 11.
Peters, T. "Opportunity Knocks," *Forbes ASAP,* June 2, 1997.

SONDRA SHAW-HARDY *directed fundraising at Western Michigan University in Kalamazoo, Michigan, before marrying and moving back to her hometown of Traverse City, Michigan, where she is cochairing a $7 million campaign for a performing arts center. She is coauthor of* Reinventing Fundraising: Realizing the Potential of Women's Philanthropy *and cofounder of the Women's Philanthropy Institute in Madison, Wisconsin. She teaches fundraising as an adjunct professor of public affairs at Western Michigan University and at Northwestern Michigan College.*

Through a structure that stressed volunteer inclusiveness, Women in Development of Greater Boston evolved from a grassroots effort to one of this country's largest professional associations for women in fundraising careers.

3

Women in Development of Greater Boston: The evolution of an organization

Phyllis S. Fanger

Women in Development is a professional membership association whose mission is to support the advancement of its members.

SO READS THE SIMPLE MISSION STATEMENT of the group that is today the largest organization of advancement professionals in New England. Since its founding in 1980 by a few development professionals, Women in Development—popularly known as WID—has matured into a vital organization of approximately eight hundred women. Through its varied programs, services, and opportunities for volunteer involvement, members help one another develop and improve professional skills, share information about employment opportunities, and foster a climate that promotes professional achievement.

NEW DIRECTIONS FOR PHILANTHROPIC FUNDRAISING, NO. 19, SPRING 1998 © JOSSEY-BASS PUBLISHERS

This striking growth in membership has been paralleled by an increasing sophistication in programming to meet the needs of a group that is diverse in age, experience, organizational affiliation, and interests.

History of WID's growth

WID's beginnings were modest indeed. In the summer of 1980, nine women who worked in development positions in colleges and universities in the Boston area met to consider holding occasional informal meetings with their peers. It was a casual meeting, and discussion centered on identifying the issues facing the growing number of women in fundraising. There was no clear focus, but the need for support from other women in a field then dominated by men was evident.

Women were not only few in number but lacked a cohesive voice within the profession. Many had little or no contact with those in other organizations. Information about the number of women employed in development or details about their position levels and salaries was nonexistent; the occasional surveys conducted by professional groups were not tabulated by gender at that time. The perception of development as an old boys' network was still dominant.

During the sixties and seventies, there had been an increasing professionalism in the field, accompanied by a demand for fundraising experience. A small but growing number of women had begun to enter development, but few had yet achieved positions of leadership. At regional conferences, with one hundred or more in attendance, it was a novelty to see more than a handful of women in a workshop meeting. But as more women joined the newly expanded staffs of higher education development offices, the annual mid-winter conferences of the Council for Advancement and Support of Education (CASE) became a meeting ground for women and their colleagues from other institutions. At the 1980 CASE District I conference in Montreal, several Boston-area women discussed the idea of forming a local support group.

In July of that year, the nine women, now fondly labeled the founding mothers of WID, first got together. They wanted to find out what data were available on women in the field, what research was under way, and what other organizations were doing about the changing demographics, that is, the greater numbers of women. Many of their concerns, reflected in the agenda of an early meeting, are still timely today: networking, skill building, salary levels, job descriptions and responsibilities, and the role of the development officer in institutional planning.

It was initially agreed to limit this new informal group to women who worked in colleges and universities in the Boston area, and the first task was to gather names. With phone calls and a mailed questionnaire to local colleagues, the first list was compiled. The organizers, now formed as a steering committee, also sought to identify any similar groups, define a logical geographic area, and consider offering job networking, career planning, teaching, and problem solving. Another interest expressed early in these discussions was conducting research to compare the progress of women with that of their male counterparts. It was clear that tackling all of these issues was a formidable challenge and that priorities would have to be established soon. Yet the enthusiasm and commitment shown by those women have remained hallmarks of the leadership of WID over the intervening years.

With little effort, word spread quickly about the new group. Requests to have names added to the mailing list flooded in. Beginning in May 1981, bimonthly breakfast meetings were held on different campuses, with the host member choosing a topic, handling the mailing, and collecting a nominal fee for refreshments. Within a few months, the list included thirty-five names; attendance was even higher, as members recruited colleagues to join them. Roundtable discussions and panels of speakers drawn from the membership were featured. Gradually the restriction of higher education employment was dropped, as women from hospital development and other sectors were added to the list. An informal custom of announcing job openings and conferences developed. Throughout the first year, two members maintained the list, collected modest dues to cover mailing costs, and circulated the list to the next meeting's host to send out notices. In those dark ages before computerized lists, this procedure soon became unmanageable, as the number approached one hundred.

About this time, a few articles and speeches about women in fundraising began to appear in the professional literature. CASE had launched a committee on career advancement for minorities and women, and other national professional associations began to take note of the growing numbers of women in their ranks. So it was logical that the concept of a local organization devoted to the needs of women in the profession would have great appeal. There was some initial resistance to creating a new association, as many women already were affiliated with established organizations such as the National Society of Fund Raising Executives (NSFRE), CASE, and the Association for Hospital Development (AHD). A few thought a new group would be competing for the involvement of busy professionals, whereas others preferred to work within the other organizations to pressure for increased attention to the interests of women. But the proponents prevailed. A well-attended meeting was held in the fall of 1982 to consider a more formal organization, with officers, a statement of purpose, and articles of organization. Over the next several months, these steps were accomplished. An executive committee made up of the president, treasurer, clerk, and five directors met often to refine the details, with bylaws defining membership, job descriptions and terms for officers, a dues structure, and specific board responsibilities. Annual dues were set at $5 but were raised to a more realistic $15 the following year. With an expanding membership of over one hundred, the board was determined to involve as many members as possible on committees—a policy that has proved to be a key ingredient in the long-term success of WID.

The identity of the new organization was clearly expressed in the statement of purpose that launched WID: "The purpose of Women in Development of Greater Boston is to establish and maintain a nonprofit professional association of women in the field of development in the Greater Boston area. Its members are committed to help one another to develop skills, share information about employment opportunities, and create a climate in which women may grow and achieve positions of increasing responsibility within the profession."

In contrast with the earlier informal roundtables and member-led panel discussions, professional speakers and meetings with a more targeted focus began to appear. An all-day mentoring seminar was the forerunner of a still-continuing theme in programming for WID members, who place a high value on access to more experienced fellow members. Among the first outside speakers was noted author Rosabeth Moss Kanter, who presented a Harvard Business School case on office politics. The spectrum of subjects offered was becoming wider.

The growing pains of a new organization were reflected in the myriad issues requiring the board's attention. Criteria for membership, increased dues and program charges, a letterhead with new logo, and fiscal stability were among standard matters to be dealt with. More challenging problems arose. For example, before filing with the state as a nonprofit, it was necessary to assure the legality of an organization open only to women. Other questions to be settled included how to expand and formalize a job information network; whether a senior woman's portfolio for top-level positions would be effective; whether to publicize the meetings of other development organizations; whether WID should seek to hold a joint meeting with a foundation officers' group of women; how to maintain the membership list efficiently. And what about a members' salary survey? In a few short years, the agenda of the fledgling organization had broadened significantly. In retrospect these early concerns were elementary, although none of those first leaders could have predicted what lay ahead for WID.

By its fourth year, WID could count 150 members, with high attendance for meetings on topics such as "Gender Differences: Women and Men at Work and Play" (offered by a psychologist), "Communications and Creative Decision Making" (from a professor of business administration), "The Next Step in Career Management" (with a human resources management specialist), and a program with two search firm executives. In the same year, a membership directory was published, and the first of nine annual salary surveys was done, with a 50 percent response rate. The survey highlighted a wide salary range ($11,400–$55,000), with an average of $25,834, and gave a snapshot of the members' employment status. Nearly three-fourths worked in education; half had been in their current job for one year or less but averaged 5.7 years in development. Later surveys used increasingly sophisticated statistical analyses and showed upward progression in salary levels as women gained more experience. In 1991, for example, the range was even wider ($17,500–$108,000), and the average salary was $38,767. Analyses were made by job title and institutional employment, and comparative figures from a survey of college and university fundraisers by the College and University Personnel Association were reprinted from *The Chronicle of Philanthropy*. However, without actual parallel data on male salaries to support or deny the suspected major gap, the WID survey was later dropped. (National organizations were by this time documenting the phenomenon of a salary gap between men and women through their surveys.) Salary surveys were nonetheless popular with WID members, who used the information to measure their own progress and to support efforts when negotiating for a new position.

Similarly, monthly job listings later became a major focus of interest and probably one of the most important reasons for many women to join WID. One of the earliest committees formed was the job resource committee, which addressed the interest in networking—long a primary raison d'être of WID. The committee's first efforts were to sponsor informal monthly breakfast meetings for job seekers, where information on openings, interviewing, and writing résumés was exchanged. A job listings notebook was made available, and members shared subjective views on the working environment at specific institutions.

Although rarely voiced publicly, there was some concern that WID was indirectly promoting a growing phenomenon of job hopping. This was balanced by the belief that women, many of whom were relatively new to the professional job market, had a basic need for assistance.

Another underlying worry about the negative side of networking was clearly expressed by an early president of WID, Ann Caldwell, when she wrote in the first issue of WID's newsletter in 1985:

The word "networking" as it has come to be used by many women troubles me, although the opportunity for networking was a central aim in establishing Women in Development of Greater Boston and a major cause of its growth. . . . I worry that networking has come to mean almost exclusively a vehicle for *individual* career advancement. "What's in it for me?" seems the underlying motive for networking. I hope Women in Development will broaden our concept of networking beyond self-interest to something economists call "collective networking." Collective networking describes a shared commitment to advance the opportunities, rewards, and working conditions for all women in a profession. Women in Development is unique among the professional organizations many of us belong to *because* it is organized by and for women in the profession. That fact gives special impetus to our programs and membership services to address issues that will help *all* women in the development field achieve a more open path to professional advancement. I am confident that Women in Development has filled a real need during its first four years and confident that as its membership grows, so too will its concept of networking.

An equally important and long-standing focus has been on mentoring. With membership growth came a wider representation of age and experience as well as job setting and specialization. Those with greater experience had different needs for programs but were seen as valuable resources by women new to development. As news about WID spread, there was also evidence of great interest among women who were just considering entering the field. To assist them, in the spring of 1985 WID created a special category of associate membership, limited to one year.

By 1984–85, with membership at 185, WID's programs began to be more varied. Four general meetings, two breakfasts, and two lunches were held. To avoid conflicts, schedules were checked with other organizations such as the Massachusetts chapter of NSFRE, CASE District I, and PGGNE (Planned Giving Group of New

England). In addition to the now-annual mentoring forum, program topics included negotiating skills, consulting, and building leadership skills for women. The latter was designed specifically for "senior" members, the definition of which has long been a subject of controversy for WID leadership. To get feedback on the value of each program, an evaluation sheet for members' reactions was introduced.

This same year marked the introduction of WID's first publication—a newsletter produced three times a year. Appearing in the first few issues were articles on the job network breakfasts, the work of a researcher, a stewardship program, a profile of the founding president, reviews of a book and of two local fundraising courses, a series of case studies, and the schedule of upcoming meetings. Although a president's column has been a regular feature, other contents have varied. The newsletter has provided an essential communication tool that brings an enhanced sense of affiliation to the now widespread membership, many of whom attend meetings only occasionally. It has also documented the work of the committees, profiled selected members, summarized programs, reported on job changes, and showcased major accomplishments. Reports of surveys on direct mail and printing firms, on fundraising software, and other practical subjects have appeared in the newsletters. The earliest issues were modest by today's editorial and graphic standards, but they created a model for useful and interesting information that has been retained. Written by volunteers, the WID newsletter seems to reflect the interests of its members and is widely read.

A period of fast growth followed. With membership in the fall of 1985 at about two hundred, the count rose to well over three hundred within a year. Size inevitably dictated changes. The format of monthly face-to-face meetings with job seekers and a circulating notebook of openings was no longer feasible, and in March 1986 the first published list of job opportunities was circulated to subscribers who paid a fee of $10 a year to cover printing and mailing costs. It was a far cry from today's ten- to twelve-page monthly listing and telephone hotline of senior, mid-career, junior, and part-time, temporary, and internship positions that the job network committee publishes. This publication's paid ads—a source of significant income for WID—is perhaps the most widely circulated item of its kind in the profession. There is no longer a subscription fee to members, all of whom receive copies; many give photocopies to others. Few employers in the Boston area, and some even far beyond Boston, who are advertising to fill positions today would omit placing an ad in the WID Job Network listing.

Changes in programming and staffing

Although the organization was a relative newcomer among associations of development professionals, WID began early to reach out to other groups for joint programming. There was a special interest in identifying other women's groups, and several conferences were held with members of WID groups from the Worcester and Springfield areas. Contacts were made with several similar women's groups across the country. One of them, Women in Financial Development of New York, extended invitations to WID's members to attend their meetings. New groups have also approached WID for help in getting started, including women in the Albany-Troy, New York, area several years ago. WID's reputation was spreading, as evidenced by its inclusion in articles in a *Chronicle of Philanthropy* feature in June 1992 on "Women's New Charity Clout," which stimulated calls from around the country for information.

In the Boston area, WID has also collaborated with NSFRE and other organizations. After first sponsoring its own celebration of National Philanthropy Day, WID became one of several sponsors of the local event. For several years, a joint calendar of programs offered locally was published. More recently, a coordinating committee with representation from several development associations has met to plan joint programs and to avoid duplication or calendar conflicts. Courses at Simmons College and Radcliffe College have been developed to provide management training for WID members.

A unique partnership was developed with The Boston Club, an organization of women holding senior management positions in Greater Boston financial services, law, marketing, and manufacturing firms. A joint committee was formed to help place women members of both groups on nonprofit boards, with mutual benefits for the organizations and the women selected.

Changes in committee structures

The source of WID's strength over the years has undoubtedly been the volunteer leaders and the committee structure. The initial committees on programs, mentoring, membership, and nominating were soon augmented by the job resource, newsletter, and public policy committees. Others were created to take on specific portfolios, such as the philanthropy award committee. Ad hoc committees were set up from time to time to address specific issues, such as a long-range planning committee, which in 1989 addressed areas of equity, membership, professional development, internal issues (programs and activities), and external issues (public policy, outreach, relationships with other organizations, and collaborative ventures). Two years later the group revisited these areas and made priority recommendations, including promotion of a multiethnic membership, ethical behavior, salary equity, professional development education, collaboration with other women's groups, volunteer services, and advocacy of leadership for women in advancement. This response to WID's dramatic growth was typical of a continuing conscientious effort, culminating in the 1993–94 strategic planning process led by a planning consultant. The board, past presidents, and a strategic planning committee collaborated in four task force groups on programs and services, governance, financial policies, and affiliations. Their findings were joined with input from a member survey and an open forum to develop a five-year plan for WID.

Volunteers have staffed these committees and devoted an extraordinary amount of time to achieving their goals. As professionals whose jobs typically involve working with volunteers, the members have been able to serve effectively as volunteers themselves. Since WID's formal organization, approximately ninety women have served on WID's board. The current board includes eighteen members, and the latest published committee rosters showed an additional total of ninety-seven. This translates into the active involvement of about one out of every eight current members.

Today's committee structure has evolved over time from the needs and interests of members and the creative approaches of the successive administrations of eight presidents and their board members. It is currently constituted of seven separate committees. The largest, the career management committee, includes four subcommittees: city service, job network, brown bag, and career workshops. In a project designed to aid small nonprofits with little or no professional development staff and no funds for consultants, the city service committee matches volunteer WID members with selected nonprofits looking for pro bono consulting services. This recently revised program has mutual benefits for participants, who gain experience in consulting or who receive professional expertise the agency could not otherwise afford. The job network subcommittee oversees the monthly job lists of advertisements. Career-related topics of interest are presented in small, informal settings by the brown bag subcommittee. These gatherings have great appeal to members and are offered at low cost compared to expensive hotel luncheon meetings. A new subcommittee on career workshops offers practical career skills programs. Collectively, these career management subcommittees are addressing many of the basic needs that WID members have articulated since the organization began.

A second committee engaged in career advancement is the equity committee, which focuses on salary equity for women as well as such issues as the feminization of fundraising and professional advancement. A negotiation hotline has offered confidential exchanges for women who are involved in salary and benefit negotiations. This strategy is an outgrowth of a 1992 WID publication, *Getting What You Deserve: A Reference Guide to Compensation and Salary Negotiation*, and several earlier workshops on negotiating.

The education committee sponsors programs for the full membership, typically on a monthly basis, and sometimes relating to a yearly theme. The chief characteristic has been a wide variety of subjects, but recent efforts have aimed at focusing programs and integrating them with other committees' offerings. Speakers come from diverse backgrounds: consultants, academics, CEOs of nonprofits, feminist authors, as well as leading development professionals. Topics are also varied, as the following titles show: "Fundraising in the Nineties and Beyond," "A New Burst of Power: Strategies for Women to Create Their Own Models for Success," "Celebrating Philanthropy," "Affirmative Action: Should We Care?," "Negotiation and Communication: The Art of the Impossible," "Collaborations, Partnerships and Mergers: Opportunity or Necessity?," "Thinking Beyond the Dollar Goal: A Capital Campaign as an Organization's 'Transforming Moment'." The breadth of subjects covered now may reflect the more complex career interests of women with longer tenure in development than was the case when WID began. A special program—the annual meeting in May—typically features an inspirational speech by a woman from the world of philanthropy or an outstanding author.

The external relations committee has the goal of helping WID gain visibility in the community and promoting its members. After many years of honoring a woman philanthropist with a WID award, the organization began to honor some of its own with Professional Leadership Awards in various categories of career accomplishment. Recently added was a New Initiatives Award for young practitioners, when three young WID members were acknowledged for creating the Young Professionals Network, an informal group within WID designed to encourage young women new to the field to get together to share fundraising ideas with peers in similar positions. The committee also writes member profiles in the newsletter and issues press releases announcing members' appointments to leadership positions in WID. Occasional member surveys are done by the external relations committee.

Membership acquisition and the newsletter are the primary jobs of the member services committee. An annual membership directory and update are issued by the committee, which also awards several membership scholarships each year. With membership at nearly eight hundred, the importance of making new members feel welcome and keeping continuing members involved requires creating new strategies so that WID's success in attracting so many women does not become a deterrent to active participation.

The nominating committee seeks to recruit candidates for office whose experience will add depth and breadth to the board and who will effectively represent the membership at large. Recently terms were restructured so that one-third of the board is chosen each year. To make the transition of the presidency a smooth one, a new position of president-elect was added. Leadership of such a large organization is central to its healthy continuity, and WID has profited from a succession of talented presidents. Each has had the essential dedication and ability to inspire others, devoting a great deal of time to WID while still managing her full-time development job.

The senior services committee is a relatively new addition, but its charge addresses a need that WID has tried to meet over the years with varying degrees of success. Initially, members sought the bonding offered by affiliating with women in the same field. Although years of professional experience and level of position varied, these differences were slight and were seen as less important than the commonality of belonging to the same field. But as membership grew, the women who attained senior-level status had less in common with those just entering development. These senior women wanted special programs to help them at that stage of their careers, where they had attained, or were positioned to move into, top advancement posts. Some of them may have felt almost besieged by the younger WID job seekers who viewed them as potential employers.

A first senior organizational management seminar was held for thirty members in 1986, and a series of seminars began in 1991. Yet creating a clear definition of a senior member posed problems. Which criteria should be used to distinguish between "senior" and other members: years of experience? job title? size of institution?

number of employees supervised? budget? Lengthy discussions ensued, and some felt that self-selection was the best option. Recently a nomination form that states established criteria was designed to allow members to self-select through an open process. The committee has designed a senior executives program, which was launched in the past year with a three-day retreat on current issues affecting senior development professionals.

Although volunteer efforts have always been at the core of everything WID has undertaken, it was recognized in the early years that some routine tasks required the daily, hands-on attention that only a paid service could provide. A list management service was hired after volunteers had maintained membership records for the first three years. Gradually other time-consuming jobs such as printing and mailing were done by outside services. The company that was hired in 1987 served a secretarial support function, maintaining WID's database, handling mailings, answering phone inquiries, and helping to produce the annual directory.

By 1989, following the board's development of a long-range plan to clarify issues and establish goals for the organization, which then represented more than five hundred women, an executive assistant was hired. The position, first conceived simply as an extra pair of hands for busy board members, has evolved into an integral part of WID's operations. Now titled managing director, Barbara Creeden is an experienced development professional and has held the sole paid staff position from the start. She is responsible for overseeing the service company that currently handles database management, inquiry resolution, job listing and directory production, monthly mailings, site arrangements for WID programs, and committee support. Her specific assignments include managing WID's finances, investments, and tax preparation; facilitating board activities; overseeing committee activities; and managing projects such as the directory and the annual report. The smooth functioning of the organization is due in large part to an effective partnership of the board and the managing director.

The financing of WID has also undergone dramatic changes during the past seventeen years, as administration and member services have expanded. A current budget of more than $128,000 could hardly have been imagined in the days when a handful of members paid $15 in annual dues. The current dues structure is $95 for members employed by nonprofits (or $145 for consultants and others in the for-profit sector).

With its membership at 750–800 in recent years, WID may anticipate a leveling off, although such predictions in the past have failed to materialize. But success cannot be measured in size alone. For an evaluation, I asked six past presidents and the current president who succeeded me to comment on WID's achievements during their terms and to offer their views on the challenges that may lie ahead.

Challenges ahead

Most frequently mentioned by the past presidents was the phenomenal growth in membership during each presidency, which some cited as not only an achievement but a problem as well. As Ann Caldwell, vice president for development at Brown University and the second president of WID, noted, "We dealt with the demands of a much more diverse membership, many of whom wanted basic training in the profession as opposed to what we on the board perceived to be our unique mission, namely advancing women in the profession and tackling the issues and barriers to that end."

Susan Galler, a consultant on nonprofit management and former senior vice president at Beth Israel Deaconess Medical Center, commented on equity as the focus of her presidency in 1986–88. It was then that the decision was made to stop the salary survey because, by surveying only members, "we were giving women lower statistics by sampling them alone." Another achievement during her term was the first joint planning meeting with the local presidents of the National Society of Fundraising Executives, the Planned Giving Group of New England, and the New England Association of Hospital Development.

The decision to hire an executive assistant, the creation of the first long-range planning committee, a retreat for new and old board members led by a facilitator, and the expansion of senior programming were identified as 1988–90's most significant achievements by WID's fourth president, Lola Baldwin, dean for external relations at Walnut Hill School. It was also a period of finding out what the enlarged membership wanted for programs, while making it clear that WID was not a "how-to" group.

Susan Paresky, chief of development at Dana-Farber Cancer Institute, who served as WID's president during 1990–92, selected the creation of the nonprofit board committee collaboration with The Boston Club as a highlight of those years, as well as the establishment of a volunteer service committee. Major issues included clarifying WID's 501(c)3 status, defining the role of various committees, creating committee budgets, and working on the definition of a senior development professional.

WID had reached its tenth year when Catherine Conover, vice president for college advancement at Wheaton College in Massachusetts, became president. A continuing issue was the management of growth, with a varied constituency and large turnover in membership. She cites as major accomplishments the completion of a successful strategic planning endeavor through focus groups and outreach, which laid a blueprint for future development of WID, and the establishment of a budgeting process, giving program managers the ability to operate within set performance expectations. Earlier collaborations with similar groups in central and western Massachusetts became less important, while strategic alliances were forged with other Boston-based development organizations to collaborate in programming. A dial-in service was added to the monthly job listings to allow timeliness and accessibility. The idea of opening membership to men was discussed, but WID's mission as an advocacy organization for women was reaffirmed.

The strategic planning process, begun during her term as vice president, enabled Carol Bonnar, president of the Philanthropic Collaborative and WID's seventh president, to implement it with focus groups convened around membership needs, diversity issues, administrative functions, and governance. She cited this achievement, which gave the board a mandate for managing WID's future direction and determining priorities for resources and services.

Most recently, President Mary Jane McGlennon, a development consultant and former director of development at the New England Aquarium, notes that the board has focused on implementing WID's mission with simplicity, clarity, and power so that more members would take an active role in their organization. Each committee and program chair and each newsletter editor was urged to make clear their connection to the mission. She also cites the progress of the city service committee and the Coalition of Professional Fundraising Organizations, both concepts initiated by earlier leaders.

These women have also done some crystal ball gazing to predict the future challenges that will face the organization. Ann Caldwell sees the changing nature of the profession and the dominance of women as key issues.

I truly believe the challenge for WID and the profession as a whole is how we deal with the increasingly technical and specialized nature of the development profession. When development professionals are viewed as technicians, we lose the opportunity to help shape the mission and priorities of the institutions we serve. At the same time, becoming more specialized and expert in our field is what has fueled the growth of the profession and the increasing demand and dependence on development programs. This isn't exactly a women's issue, but it could lead to a devaluing of the profession in which women are now the majority. The other challenge is how to attract more men to the profession. The pendulum may have swung as far as we would want it to; as more women are becoming managers and therefore hiring others, we need to be careful not to hire only people just like us (i.e., other women!). That's what the old boy network did, which kept women out of the profession in the old days!

Susan Galler focuses on the need for a coalition of women to address the larger issues of philanthropy and women, as a challenge to WID: "I think that WID's challenge for the future is to be a catalyst for a collaborative working model among women trustees, foundation officers, women advisors and donors. There's a vital role for WID to play in convening women together to strengthen philanthropy for women. The next agenda is to have women's money and expertise further the women's agenda."

Some key organizational issues draw Lola Baldwin's attention as challenges for the future. She writes, "The challenges will be keeping programs relevant to the broad spectrum of skills and levels in the membership, especially seniors; communicating with membership on WID and development issues; finding good leaders; and continuing to keep in touch with what the membership wants— senior programming is always an issue."

Susan Paresky mentions a variety of membership and programmatic subjects that will demand WID's special attention in the future:

Bringing men into the system and up the career ladder is a huge and growing problem. What to do with seniors will always remain a problem, and another challenge will be to keep membership educated on technical and regulatory changes in a timely fashion. Keeping program costs down and program quality up is always an issue. Other issues include competition from NSFRE and securing top-rated speakers, which is always a problem. In the future, how should WID train/educate/promote women as expert managers and leaders? How should WID manage the explosive growth in philanthropy? How should WID manage the need for specific area training which has become much more focused and technical?

Growth and evolution are the keywords chosen by Catherine Conover as challenges for the future, and she adds, "Finding a voice for WID that is heard beyond our membership, and perhaps beyond our industry, has not been fully successful. I suspect we are a reflection of some of the ambivalence many women in the profession are feeling; and we need to help find solutions to job burnout, management of expectations, and some of the other key issues that if not addressed will ultimately damage our fundraising efforts."

Looking ahead to future educational needs in development, Carol Bonnar comments, "Providing high quality training to meet future trends in philanthropy is a distinct challenge. What is WID's future role in training professionals to meet the needs of a global economy? What credentials and education are necessary? Who will provide it? What collaborations make sense?"

Leading the challenge of a changing profession are the words chosen by Mary Jane McGlennon to describe WID's future charge. She says, "Many people ask me if WID's mission has been achieved, with women now dominating the field and holding a large share of the most senior positions. The answer is a resounding "no." While we must address the issues of diversity in the field, including the reentry of men, as our profession becomes more complex so does the professional advancement of women. When WID was first formed, the vision of a women's fundraising organization was unusual, exciting, and daring. Today's challenge is to build on the success and stability of the past while recreating that sense of excitement."

As the founding president of WID, I have been awed by its transition from an informal caucus of women seeking support from other women to a large association offering a panoply of programs and services to hundreds of ambitious and accomplished women at all levels of the profession. The power of an idea in the hands of dedicated women can never be underestimated.

PHYLLIS S. FANGER *retired after thirty years in higher education development at institutions including Wellesley College, Brandeis University, and Northeastern University. She was founding president of Women in Development of Greater Boston.*

As efforts to advance fundraising's professionalism gain momentum and attention from practitioners and theorists, equity issues in compensation and position are key aspects of developing practice and policy guidelines in the future.

4

Gender and pay equity in the fundraising workforce: Implications for practice and policy

Julie C. Conry

AS WOMEN continue to flock to fundraising positions across all nonprofit organizations in the United States, they have achieved, in the last ten years, a majority in the memberships of the top three professional organizations representing fundraisers: The National Society of Fund Raising Executives (NSFRE), the Council for the Advancement and Support of Education (CASE), and the Association for Healthcare Philanthropy (AHP).

Based on the periodic surveys these associations have produced after tracking and measuring their members during the last decade, the current profile of the occupational shifts in fundraising that emerges continues to evoke a wide range of opinions regarding the role of gender.

Within the framework of identifying fundraising as an occupation that is more and more gender-dominant or feminized, that is,

NEW DIRECTIONS FOR PHILANTHROPIC FUNDRAISING, NO. 19, SPRING 1998 © JOSSEY-BASS PUBLISHERS

more women than men are entering it as paid employees, some key issues surround the gender question as practitioners, managers, consultants, and donors react and respond to the changes at hand. Most striking is that despite their noticeable gains in number in a period when market demand for fundraisers is high, women fundraisers have not made equal progress in compensation rates and organizational position. Further, there is growing evidence that within certain fundraising specialties, women are now occupationally segregated, filling 75 to 100 percent of the positions.

The current discrepancy in salaries between men and women in the fundraising workforce bears examination on several fronts. Pay equity was an issue in the U.S. labor market long before the Equal Pay Act of 1963 made sex-based wage discrimination illegal. Study after study has documented that, even with legislation, in the intervening years the earnings ratio between men and women has improved incrementally (Jaussaud, 1984). Census Bureau data continue to show both men and women still earning lower wages in woman-dominated fields ("Briefing Paper #1: The Wage Gap," 1989). As efforts to advance fundraising's professionalism gain momentum and attention from practitioners and theorists, equity issues in compensation and position are key aspects of this struggle. Equity imbalances are not likely to be totally self-correcting. The complexity of defining the root of the problems and proposing solutions applicable to all will require sustained attention for some time to come.

A variety of commentators have rationalized the pay gap in fundraising as a function of age, experience level, and the clustering of women at entry-level positions, which have increased rapidly since the mid-1980s. Some cite personal characteristics as mitigating factors: women who won't, don't, or can't negotiate for parity or who demand little and settle for less. Some suggest that organizational barriers keep women from achieving top management posts, creating an uneven distribution of women in technical and staff positions where compensation rates are lower and opportunities for advancement are more limited. Others point to the entrepreneurial climate of fundraising as rewarding those who have self-selected in and have the talent and resources to succeed in a competitive venue, regardless of credentials, or who have had the good fortune to link up with a seasoned mentor at crucial career stages.

There are clearly differing theories, limited consensus, and many personal histories that point to a variety of complex factors contributing to pay gap scenarios. With the rapid influx of women in fundraising likely to continue in the near future, do issues such as career paths, economic equity, and professionalization have particular relevance to women building fundraising portfolios? What are the significant income predictors for fundraisers? How can pay disparity be addressed to preserve occupational integrity and minimize the gender penalty?

These questions must frame any discussion of the demographic and operational trends now occurring in fundraising as it continues its shift toward a predominantly female workforce.

Women in the fundraising workforce, 1985–1995

The last decade in fundraising has been marked not only by the significant numbers of women choosing fundraising as a career but also by an increased scrutiny of what the numbers mean to the growth and status of an emerging profession.

A gradual but consistent trend over the last ten years has been documented by the official tracking mechanisms among the three main professional associations that represent fundraisers—the annual or periodic surveys that collect data on items such as compensation, titles, experience, working conditions, and credentials. Women are being absorbed into the fundraising workforce by the thousands—a migration that has generated mixed interpretations about gender's role in a field that historically was limited in its gender and racial diversity.

The demographics indicate the following:

- Membership in the National Society of Fund Raising Executives (NSFRE) jumped from 5,000 to 16,000 between 1984 and 1995.

In 1988 women made up 52 percent of the membership; by 1992 they were a 57.6 majority—a figure that held steady in the 1995 survey (Greene and Murawski, 1996; Mixer, 1994; "Profile 1988: NSFRE Career Survey," 1988).

- Membership in the Council for the Advancement and Support of Education (CASE), which represents higher education, indicates women's enrollment rose from 48.5 percent in 1986 to 54.7 percent in 1989, then leveled off to 53.6 percent in 1995 (Conry, 1991; Williams, 1996).

- Membership in the Association for Healthcare Philanthropy (formerly the National Association for Hospital Development) indicates that women are now 55 percent of the membership, up from 42 percent in 1987 (Association for Healthcare Philanthropy, 1995).

The profile of the "typical" advancement professional has shifted. CASE, in 1986, described its average member as a "white male employed as a director of development or advancement at a private, coeducational, four-year college or university" ("The 1985 CASE Survey of Institutional Advancement," 1986).

By 1995, it was reported that "the quintessential CASE member is female, holds the title of director, is in her early 40s, with more than 10 years of advancement experience" (Williams, 1996, p. 10). In health care fundraising, the picture is similar. The average AHP member is female, in her mid-forties, with nine years of experience and holds a college degree (Association for Healthcare Philanthropy, 1995).

NSFRE describes its typical member in 1995 as female, median age of forty, with a college degree and seven years of fundraising experience (Mongon, 1996).

Both trade and popular media stories documenting the increasing numbers of women moving into fundraising cite similar reasons for the current popularity and attraction of fundraising as a career destination: high salary potential, the opportunity to work for causes that have social acceptance and value, the emphasis on bottom-line results, the increasing reliance of nonprofits on private gifts to augment traditional sources of support, and an alignment with volunteerism. The emerging activism and visibility of women philanthropists and their perceived influence to ultimately direct significant charitable funds in the coming decades is also viewed as an element that works in favor of women fundraisers (Hall, 1992; Shaw and Taylor, 1995).

In 1990, *Working Woman* magazine listed "development officer" as one of the twenty most promising occupations for women in the 1990s. The reasons cited were the increasing demand of a wide range of organizations to raise charitable dollars, the greater use of big business marketing tools, and the chances to make, after ten years, salaries between $60,000 and $90,000 (Russell, 1990).

A later story in *Working Woman*, "Asking for a Fortune," declared fundraising a "hot ticket" for women, particularly those seeking meaningful work and satisfaction that eluded them in corporate environments. As a mission-driven career option, fundraising was described as offering clear goals, advancement based on results, and work performance that was quantifiable (Tifft, 1992).

In addition to this mix of congruent values and expanding opportunity is the "skills" dimension—that because the foundation of fundraising is based on interpersonal relations, people giving to people for purposes that are noble, some women are now transferring skills they had historically donated to causes into paid positions. Another recurring theme in explaining the appeal of fundraising to women is the perception that as society's designated nurturers, women are, by virtue of their gender, uniquely equipped to excel and be accepted in a people-oriented business.

Whether their motivations are altruistic, economic, academic, or value-driven, in the rapid ten-year rise from minority to majority, women have taken a foothold and established a notable presence in the fundraising arena. They now occupy all fundraising job categories, and they work in a vast matrix of nonprofit organizations, educational institutions, health care centers, and consulting firms. They play key roles in campaigns—in planning, organizing, soliciting, and advising donors and volunteers. They have established networks and associations for women fundraisers and women philanthropists, both formally and informally. They have assumed leadership positions in the professional groups designated to represent fundraisers such as CASE, the NSFRE, and the AAFRC.

Yet their growth in numbers and proficiency has been tempered by persistent pay gaps and slow and uneven professional advancement. It is a good-news-bad-news scenario. Even though overall salaries are climbing for fundraisers, women's pay is consistently lagging behind that of men. Women holding senior management positions in fundraising are still a fraction of their overall numbers as a group, and in some job classifications women are filling virtually all the positions. Rapid turnover rates continue to be the norm, as career advancement is tied more and more to moving out instead of moving up.

These developments are particularly compelling, in part, for their resonance. During the late 1980s, as the clarion call went out to address issues of gender and fundraising practice, three assumptions were debated: whether, as fundraising becomes a profession dominated by women, the resulting feminization will (1) lower salaries, (2) cluster women in technical-skills positions instead of management, and (3) reduce status and prestige.

How have these assumptions, in the mid-1990s, crystallized? In the areas of compensation and position, women fundraisers, as a group, appear to be paying a gender penalty, contrary to other encouraging and outward signs of progress. The survey data indicate that women in fundraising, like their female colleagues in other fields, have made and are making less money than men in their chosen occupation.

The salary gap

The continuing efforts of women in fundraising to reach parity and their increasing representation in the fundraising field has parallels in the larger workforce. Women are 51 percent of the U.S. population; they are 46 percent of the workforce; they now receive 55 percent of bachelor's degrees and 54 percent of master's degrees.

They are 35 percent of new physicians and 45 percent of new lawyers. In earnings, women now make 71 cents to the dollar earned by men. Among younger workers aged twenty-five to thirty-four, the gap drops to 82 cents on the dollar. One in four American workers is now employed by a woman-owned business. Women are 60 percent of the workforce in service jobs and 64 percent in technical, sales, and administrative support (Blair, 1996). In the nonprofit sector, it is estimated that women make up two-thirds to three-fourths of the employees (Preston, 1994).

As a group, professional and managerial women are leading the workforce in wage growth; in some professions, such as insurance sales and the law, women are narrowing the wage gap twice as fast as the penny-a-year rate registered overall in the last two decades (Harris, 1995).

A counterpoint to what some see as progress in closing the gender wage gap is what some analysts call an "illusion" created by men's falling salaries. Gains in women's wages were only one-third of the overall narrowing in male-female earnings between 1979 and 1993, according to economists Lawrence Mishel and Jared Bernstein of the Washington D.C.-based Economic Policy Institute. The rest is attributed to the general decline in men's wages, which made women's progress seem more significant (Harris, 1995).

In fundraising, wage growth has occurred in tandem with the continued strength of the market for professional fundraisers in the nonprofit sector. A recent INDEPENDENT SECTOR report predicted that looming congressional spending cuts would require many nonprofits to boost private donations by more than 70 percent annually to make up for the loss of federal revenue (Stehle, 1995). Many charities that historically sought private support through only volunteer networks or sporadic campaigns managed by outside consultants are adding full-time professionals. In 1992, when the climate for many charities was one of downsizing, eighty-three of the ninety-three nonprofit executives surveyed by the Development Resource Group in New York said they had hired a fundraiser in the past year, and almost half were newly created positions (Moore, 1992).

Has increased opportunity brought increased cost to women in fundraising careers? By filling many of the newly created entry-level jobs and the expanding technical support roles in fundraising, are they becoming segregated by gender, which in turn depresses salary levels? Can this account for part of the reported pay disparities between men and women? A review of the most recent salary data, income predictors, and pay differentials offers some ideas about economic equity and the fundraising workforce.

Survey findings

In the past decade, a number of surveys have documented that women in fundraising have made less money than their male counterparts, and even as their occupational participation increased, pay gaps have persisted. Gender as a variable and statistical marker is now standard in the three main association surveys: CASE, AHP, and NSFRE. The survey methodology used by the groups—questionnaires mailed to randomly selected association members—yields response rates anywhere from 40 to 70 percent, which some analysts interpret as more suggestive than conclusive. How representative these professional associations are of the total fundraising workforce is also a matter of debate, as many small nonprofit organizations ask employees to assume fundraising tasks as part of their overall responsibilities, not as a primary job focus.

Overall findings of the professional association surveys have been fairly consistent, however, in documenting a relationship between pay and gender. The 1995 NSFRE survey released in March 1996 (Mongon, 1996) reported the following:

- Men's median salary stayed relatively flat in the last three years, at $53,000; pay for women rose to $44,900 from $41,200—a gender-based difference of $8,100. In 1992, the gender difference was $12,000—women earned $40,000 to men's $52,000 average.
- At the highest salary levels, approximately 11 percent of the men earned between $75,000 and $90,000, whereas only 5 percent of

women were in that bracket. About 8 percent of the men earned between $90,000 and $115,000; for women, 2.5 percent earned that much. Nearly one-fifth of the women respondents earned between $25,000 and $40,000.

- Within specialty areas, men in the Annual Fund averaged $47,900 to women's $35,300; in Major Gifts, men earned a median of $48,700 to women's $47,500; in planned giving, men's median was $53,600 to women's $42,500; in Corporate/Foundation Relations, women's median was $45,000 to men's $43,800.

- Gender clustering, or segregation by specialty, also continues to be a trend. Women fill 68 percent of the Annual Fund positions, 59 percent of Corporate/Foundation Relations positions, 69 percent of Major Gifts, 63 percent of Grants, 100 percent of Prospect Research positions, 81 percent of Special Events, and 85 percent of Communications positions.

One cross-survey comparison of the same fundraising specialty areas suggests the disproportionate number of females clustered in certain positions has resulted in wage stagnation for these areas. A 1993 Abbott Langer survey of nonprofits indicated either salary decreases or no growth in annual fund positions, grant writing, corporate or foundation directors (salaries decreased 8 percent), and prospect research (salaries decreased 6 percent). In planned giving, which NSFRE listed as 70 percent male, a 12 percent increase in salary levels was noted (Greene and Murawski, 1996, p. 38).

These gender and salary patterns suggest that, in part, the clustering of women within certain fundraising specialty areas is contributing to the creation of what sociologist Barbara Reskin terms the female "ghetto"—lower-paid enclaves occupied almost exclusively by women within otherwise integrated organizations that follows the shift of male workers to higher-paying, more rewarding positions (Cowan, 1989).

Parity in pay within the NSFRE membership occurs mainly at the highest levels, where 18 percent of the men and 9 percent of the women report having the title of vice president. Women within this group earn a median salary of $74,200, which is $3,600 more than the men's median of $70,600. This contrast deserves further study to identify what factors, such as superior negotiating skills, experience levels, and performance record, might contribute to this difference.

Within higher education advancement and fundraising, the 1995 CASE survey outlines a statistical picture similar to the NSFRE findings. It concluded that overall salaries rose by 26.9 percent between 1990 and 1995, from a median of $41,981 to $53,262. Women have narrowed the salary gap by four cents, from 74 cents on the dollar to 78 cents, typical of the penny-a-year national average. In absolute terms, however, survey author Roger Williams noted that the 1990 pay gap between men and women of $13,000 was the same five years later, across the profession and all institutional types (Williams, 1996).

For those in advancement whose primary responsibility is fundraising, the mean salary for men was $61,568 and for women $48,209. For managers of advancement programs, the male mean was $77,500, for women $61,533. In a finding that has been repeated in two previous CASE surveys, when a multiple regression analysis was used in the 1995 data to hold all variables except gender equal—experience, age, title, degree—a big difference in salaries between women and men is related to gender alone.

Women receive lower salaries within every job title except coordinator, in every professional area except student recruitment, and at every type of institution. At two-year colleges the gap is smallest. Women make $1,765 less than men; at four-year colleges the gap is largest—$18,867.

In the health care arena, compensation has shown less robust growth—a 3.8 percent increase since 1993 in the median salary, which rose from $60,000 to $62,300, according to the 1995 Total Compensation Report of the Association for Healthcare Philanthropy (1995). This report, a Towers Perrin survey of 795 AHP members, disclosed total pay for male respondents was nearly 45.3 percent higher than for female respondents. The median salary for men was $77,000 and for women $53,000—a difference of $24,000.

Median salaries by position title and gender showed the following:

- Of those with the title of chief development officer, men averaged $83,000 to women's $57,000.
- Of those with the title of senior development officer, men averaged $70,000 to women's $54,000.
- Of those with the title of director of planned giving, men averaged $78,000 to women's $58,000.
- Of those with the title of development officer, women averaged $43,000, slightly ahead of the $42,000 male average.

In the Towers Perrin analysis, the variables that most significantly influenced pay levels in health care fundraising were annual revenue (as it relates to size and comprehensiveness) of the employing institution, gender, and years of experience. Those with fifteen or more years of experience reported incomes 94 percent higher than those with five years of experience—an indicator that, for fundraisers, longevity is a positive factor in establishing credibility and market value.

The most significant income predictors for NSFRE respondents listed in the 1995 survey were success rates in meeting annual fundraising goals; size and type of institution employing the fundraiser (highest earners worked for hospitals or educational institutions); years of experience in fundraising; job stability and low turnover levels; and education level. Although gender was used in salary comparisons, it was not listed in the survey as an income predictor.

In higher education, gender was among the most significant income predictors for fundraisers as summarized in the 1995 CASE survey. In the CASE analysis, the gender gap's complexity was partially attributed to women not being well represented at the highest management levels, being younger than the men surveyed, and being clustered disproportionately at institutions with the lowest salary levels—two-year colleges and independent schools.

Other income predictors of significance included title, type and size of institution, experience (those with less than two years made an average of $38,899; those with more than fifteen made $66,000), age, and education (those with doctoral and law degrees made the most). In 1995, the age bracket with the greatest gender disparity was the 50–59-year-olds, where men earned $17,229 more. At the highest experience levels, women with more than fifteen years in advancement made an average of $58,569 to the $71,782 made by men with the same experience levels.

These data suggest that women in fundraising do obtain less of an economic return for their years of experience, the working titles and levels of responsibility they achieve, and their selection of specialty areas within fundraising. As an occupational income predictor, being female appears to influence compensation negatively in fundraising.

With diminished economic gains have come diminished expectations on the part of some women fundraisers. In this instance, self-perceptions are revealing and could be construed as contributing factors to the status and pay issues. Roughly 17.5 percent of the women who participated in the 1995 CASE survey indicated their chances for promotion were above average or better, compared to nearly 23 percent of the men surveyed. Almost 43 percent of the women saw their chances for professional advancement as below average or poor, compared to 38.9 percent of the men. Less than half of the women (45.5 percent) said they wanted to stay in their current positions, citing job dissatisfaction as the main reason. Other reasons noted for lack of career development were limited career ladder, working in a one-person office, and prevailing stability in upper positions, producing few chances for promotion.

These assessments deserve further study to investigate how perceived institutional barriers may dictate career patterns and limit professional growth for women fundraisers, thus contributing to wage inequities and occupational segregation in technical specialty and support areas. With so many women now filling entry-level fundraising positions, it is an opportune time to institute a long-term tracking system for this cohort to gather data about how the interplay of personal and organizational characteristics influences career paths and success levels.

Models and rationales

In contemporary economic theory, researchers are in agreement that the proportion of women clustered in occupations different from men is a key factor in explaining the universal male-female wage gap. The wage gap statistics, touted in annual announcements by various government entities that women now make so many cents to every dollar a man earns, continue to be a standard benchmark for measuring women's status and progress in the labor market. The gap has been closing at a rate of about one penny a year, and across disciplines scholars pursue their quest to find more exact cause-and-effect relationships. They concede the gap is real, and most debate centers on cause, particularly within occupations rather than across occupations.

In the human capital model, theorists suggest that women invest less in acquiring labor market skills because they anticipate working fewer years, have a weaker attachment to the workforce, and have higher rates of turnover due to family responsibilities. Some economists estimate gender differences in the accumulation of human capital, the occupations men and women select, and levels of turnover account for a significant portion of the wage gap (Barron, Black, and Loewenstein, 1993).

Researchers Beller and England suggest employees practice demand-side discrimination, whereas Becker and Olson argue that women face more stringent promotion standards than men, limiting wage growth (Barron, Black, and Loewenstein, 1993). Groshen (1991) postulates that the largest source of the female-male wage gap is the association between wages and the proportion of females in the occupation. She notes that in the decade since the enactment of the very policies formulated to address segregation—EEO, affirmative action, and equal education—the gender wage gap has declined slightly but remained large.

Further, her research supports other studies that show no more than 50 percent of the gender wage gap can be attributed to factors in the human capital model, such as differences in the education, skill, training, and personal resources men and women bring to the labor force. Kelly (1991) concurs in *The Gendered Economy* that "variations in individual characteristics have seldom been able to explain more than 50 percent of gender-based pay inequities" (p. 50). The argument that a large part of the wage gap is due to women's interruptions in work for family reasons (thought to reduce skills and employability), or differences in the qualifications of men and women workers, was not borne out in a recent government studies of male-female earnings differences ("Briefing Paper #1: The Wage Gap," 1989). The studies pointed to labor market structure and unknown factors, which include sex-based wage discrimination, to explain the wage gap.

Jaussaud (1984) argues similarly that legislation aimed at reducing pay inequities has not produced statistically significant results, and it is job evaluation systems that can be designed and used to correct pay inequities between women and men. Further, Jaussaud adds that because these systems were developed and manipulated by management to serve strategic needs, they have been and continue to be used as instruments of discrimination.

Needleman and Nelson (1988) also present evidence that studies of job evaluation systems have confirmed a male bias, particularly in use and value of certain skills, such as contact with the public, managing social relations, and caretaking and caregiving.

Within these theoretical choices, women in fundraising appear to be challenged by a myriad of factors in reaching pay and position equity, including the "unknown" contributors such as sex-based wage discrimination. As the survey findings over the past decade indicate, gender remains a consistent and negative income predictor, limiting the applicability of the human capital model in explaining income disparities between male and female fundraisers.

Although some of the gaps appear to be narrowing at entry-level positions such as development officer, additional study is needed to track the advancement paths of these men and women to see if discrepancies increase or decrease, and to what degree, as their careers progress. Particularly relevant information to assess in such a study would be access to training needed for professional advancement, mentoring opportunities, credentialing, job interruptions or changes, job evaluation systems, and wage histories.

Implications for practice and policy

For those subscribing to the legitimacy of gender issues, diversity, and pay equity as relevant to fundraising's emerging professionalization, an agenda of further study and action is timely and appropriate. Given the complexity of the wage-gender scenario, a conclusive explanation of the problem will be elusive and speculative until more detailed data are collected and analyzed that crosses all professional groups. Current surveys, with their mix of variables and differing degrees of sophistication in interpreting findings, have provided adequate baseline data for tracking demographic changes. But within the profession of fundraising more is needed—more focus groups, more case studies, more personal histories—to delve deeper into what qualitative factors are now influencing the work life and compensation of the practitioner. And in the majority of organizations and institutions today, that practitioner is a woman. Any proposed policy to systematically address diversity and professionalization will fall short without more consensus and, more important, awareness that there is a problem concerning gender, fundraising roles, salaries, and status. Job evaluation systems in fundraising, for example, is an area where a comprehensive study could be very instrumental in identifying potential areas of bias, shifting values, and conflict points between employer expectations and employee performance. As pressure increases to hire fundraisers as paid, professional solicitors targeting the realm of major gifts, there is already acknowledgment within some organizations of a management preference for eager generalists with limited experience who can be "trained" in-house and will exchange the chance for experience for lower wages (Hall and Murawski, 1995; Moore, 1992). In the words of one recruitment consultant: "Charities are asking us to look outside the ranks of development professionals because they have seen the baggage that so often comes from development officers cycling through jobs—a lot of flurry and no substance" (Hall and Murawski, 1995, p. 23).

For fundraisers attempting to build credibility, compile credentials and performance records, and attain economic parity with peers, such news is disturbing and potentially detrimental to efforts to advance the profession's standing. In the absence of licensing standards, minimum educational requirements, or standardized evaluation systems, search and hiring practices for fundraisers will remain a problematic area—a zone where organizational need and expectations drive the process, and the practitioner bears significant individual responsibility to broker a successful match.

In recent years, suggested parameters to navigate this zone and proposed remedies to address pay and position inequities have included encouraging organizations to create formalized mentoring systems for women, setting up accessible programs to help them develop job and salary negotiating skills, strengthening the ethical and value base of fundraising, expanding educational and training opportunities, and improving the image of fundraising as a profession (Hall, 1992). Some have characterized the salary gap as a "temporary" problem that will fade as women accumulate experience. Others point to pending legal actions against discriminatory practices in various institutions across the country as proof that individuals are pursuing corrective action on a case-by-case basis rather than collectively (Greene and Murawski, 1996).

One program model, the Women in Development organization based in Boston (see Chapter Three), has incorporated a number of methods to assist members in raising awareness and achieving parity in pay and position. Since its founding in 1980 by a small group of professional women fundraisers, the association has grown to more than eight hundred women, and it is now the largest organization of advancement professionals in New England. The organization implemented not only a mentoring program that matches senior women professionals with those new to fundraising, it also distributes job listings, a directory, and a newsletter; in 1992 it published a formal reference guide to compensation and salary negotiation entitled "Getting What You

Deserve"—a step-by-step outline including sample scripts, bibliography references, career services information, and salary survey data (Women in Development, 1992).

A recent addition to their programming has been the creation of a job negotiation hotline; practitioners in the process of finalizing a job or position change can speak directly to senior professionals about issues like compensation, benefits, and negotiation strategies. This comprehensive program has been designed not just as a service to members but to enable women fundraisers to "help one another develop and improve professional skills, share information about employment opportunities, and foster a climate which promotes professional achievement" (Women in Development, 1992). Its design is fundamental and replicable, and by any measure it has been successful in addressing the concerns and practice issues of its core membership—women in fundraising.

In reflecting on twenty-six years in development, the first president and one of the founders of the Women in Development association, Phyllis S. Fanger, notes there is still much to be done to assure equity for women fundraisers: "Women are not yet on an equal footing with men in top management in development. Our strength is in the numbers, but the perception is not yet widespread that women can handle the top positions. . . . On the way up, women are too often given roles that are out of the spotlight, have lower gift dollar potential, or are gender-defined. These can become ghettos" (Women in Development, 1992).

Her advice to women seeking careers in fundraising—choose jobs and training carefully and wisely, invest in one's own career, negotiate for a meaningful title, network, learn from knowledgeable people, and be known by others—is a viewpoint advocating considerable personal action and assertiveness in achieving career advancement and success. One woman's path, in this case, can be a useful guide for others to follow.

But reaching true equity in pay and position for women in fundraising will also require much more than personal commitment and vigilance on the part of practitioners. At minimum, the continued attention to and appraisal of gender and diversity issues by those professional associations charged with representing fundraisers is necessary to develop effective dialogue, policies, and possible solutions. Within a sector where the majority of the workforce is now female, nonprofit theorists, researchers, and analysts can hardly afford not to incorporate aspects of gender into contemporary studies. Given its proper place, gender, as an issue, has considerable potential to generate both a greater understanding of the present dynamics of the fundraising labor market and the future status of the profession.

References

Association for Healthcare Philanthropy. "1995 Total Compensation Report-USA." Falls Church, Va.: Association for Healthcare Philanthropy, July 1995, pp. 1–12.

Barron, J. M., Black, D. A., and Loewenstein, M. A. "Gender Differences in Training, Capital and Wages." *Journal of Human Resources*, 1993, *28* (2), 343–364.

Blair, A. K. "Education and Pay Data Suggest Women Nearing Parity with Men." *Columbus Dispatch*, May 13, 1996, p. 7A.

"Briefing Paper #1: The Wage Gap." Washington, D.C.: National Committee on Pay Equity, Institute for Women's Policy Research, Apr. 1989.

Conry, J. C. "The Feminization of Fund Raising." In D. F. Burlingame and L. J. Hulse (eds.), *Taking Fund Raising Seriously: Advancing the Profession and Practice of Raising Money*. San Francisco: Jossey-Bass, 1991.

Cowan, A. "Women's Gains on the Job: Not Without a Heavy Toll." *New York Times*, Aug. 21, 1989, p. A14.

Greene, S. G., and Murawski, J. "New Faces in Fund Raising." *Chronicle of Philanthropy*, Mar. 21, 1996, pp. 37–38.

Groshen, E. "The Structure of the Female/Male Wage Differential." *Journal of Human Resources*, 1991, *26* (3), 457–472.

Hall, H. "Women's New Charity Clout." *Chronicle of Philanthropy*, June 16, 1992, p. 1.

Hall, H., and Murawski, J. "Fund Raising: Hot Career or Hot Seat?" *Chronicle of Philanthropy*, June 29, 1995, p. 1.

Harris, D. "The 16th Annual Salary Survey." *Working Woman*, Jan. 1995, pp. 25–34.

Jaussaud, D. P. "Can Job Evaluation Systems Help Determine the Comparable Worth of Male and Female Occupations?" *Journal of Economic Issues*, 1984, *18* (2), 473–480.

Kelly, R. M. *The Gendered Economy*. Thousand Oaks, Calif.: Sage, 1991.

Mixer, J. R. "Women as Professional Fundraisers." In T. Odendahl and M. O'Neill (eds.), *Women and Power in the Nonprofit Sector*. San Francisco: Jossey-Bass, 1994.

Mongon, G. J. "NSFRE Profile–1995 Membership Survey." Report of the NSFRE Foundation. Washington, D.C.: National Society of Fund Raising Executives, Mar. 18, 1996.

Moore, J. "Even in a Tight Non-Profit Job Market, Fund Raisers Have Little Trouble Finding Work." *Chronicle of Philanthropy*, Apr. 21, 1992, p. 30.

Needleman, R., and Nelson, A. "Policy Implications: The Worth of Women's Work." In A. Statham, E. Miller, and H. O. Mauksch (eds.), *The Worth of Women's Work*. New York: State University of New York Press, 1988.

"The 1985 CASE Survey of Institutional Advancement." *CASE Currents*, June 1986, pp. 8–20.

Preston, A. "Women in the Nonprofit Labor Market." In T. Odendahl and M. O'Neill (eds.), *Women and Power in the Nonprofit Sector*. San Francisco: Jossey-Bass, 1994.

"Profile 1988: NSFRE Career Survey," *NSFRE Journal*, Winter 1988, p. 22.

Russell, A. "Top 20 Careers." *Working Woman*, July 1990, p. 79.

Shaw, S. C., and Taylor, M. A. *Reinventing Fundraising: Realizing the Potential of Women's Philanthropy*. San Francisco: Jossey-Bass, 1995.

Stehle, V. "Federal Cuts 'Terrifying' for Charities." *Chronicle of Philanthropy*, June 29, 1995, p. 25.

Tifft, S. E. "Asking for a Fortune." *Working Woman*, Nov. 1992, pp. 66–94.

Williams, R. L. "Advancement's Steady Advance." *CASE Currents*, Feb. 1996, pp. 8–22.

Women in Development. "Getting What You Deserve: A Reference Guide to Compensation and Salary Negotiation." Boston: Women in Development, 1992.

JULIE C. CONRY *is director of development, The Ohio State University Health Sciences Center/College of Nursing. A graduate of Oberlin College and former Kiplinger Fellow at Ohio State, she writes, lectures, and conducts workshops and seminars on nonprofit fundraising issues, proposal development, and corporate and foundation giving.*

The opportunity to reclaim the valuable voice and presence of women in the religious philanthropic arena has never been greater.

5

Reclaiming a heritage and tradition: Women as fundraisers and leaders in religious philanthropy

Jennifer M. Goins, Janette E. McDonald

MORE THAN ANY OTHER TIME in history, women today have the opportunity to influence philanthropy and assume more authority in fundraising efforts, especially in funding for religious organizations and social causes. In order to provide a context of understanding, we examine trends in religious giving and the financial state of religious organizations. We also address the changing socioeconomic role of women and society.

Women as philanthropists for faith-based organizations, especially in the Christian tradition, have made and will continue to make a tremendous impact on the moral and physical welfare of society in the United States. To support this claim we present a historical review of documented fundraising activities from the past century. The status of women as current leaders in philanthropy will also be addressed, with some projections for future activities. Finally, the role of trusteeship in religious organizations will be discussed in relation to women's influence in religious philanthropy.

NEW DIRECTIONS FOR PHILANTHROPIC FUNDRAISING, NO. 19, SPRING 1998 © JOSSEY-BASS PUBLISHERS

Financial trends in religious organizations

Although religion consistently ranks number one among charities in the giving sweepstakes—a whopping 46 percent of $151 billion given in 1996 (*Giving USA 1997*, 1997)—the picture is by no means all rosy for churches and religious organizations. Robert Wuthnow, professor of sociology and director of the Center for the Study of American Religion at Princeton University, under a grant from the Lilly Endowment conducted a five-year extensive survey that looked at, among other socioeconomic variables, attitudes and behavior regarding faith and money (Wuthnow, 1996).

After hundreds of in-depth interviews with clergy and people from many different occupations, faiths, and ethnic backgrounds all across the United States, Wuthnow (1997) writes, "The economic prosperity that once characterized American religious institutions is now a thing of the past, and financial woes are the order of the day" (p. 46). This situation is paradoxical because *Giving USA 1997* still reports religion as the top-ranking charity in the United States. It is even more perplexing in light of a recent Gallup Poll indicating that two-thirds of Americans maintain an affiliation with a church or synagogue, and six in ten consider religion to be of high importance to their personal lives (Newport and Saad, 1998).

Despite the fact that dollars increased almost 5 percent (2 percent when adjusted for inflation), Wuthnow's study found that giving to a church as a proportion of family income has steadily declined over the past twenty years. Considering that this population is the vertebra of religious organizations throughout the United States, and that the average family income has barely held steady over the last fifteen years, clergy concern over dwindling resources is understandable. The problem is not just perceived—it is real (Wuthnow, 1997).

Although religion still dominates the percentage of donated dollars, it has in a sense lost market share. *Giving USA 1997* reports that for the last thirty years, contributions to faith-based charities and congregations accounted for 50 percent of total giving. In recent years this figure has hovered around 45 percent, indicating a 5 percent decline. In addition, cutbacks in government-sponsored social programs mandate that churches be asked to do more. Clergy are frustrated because the resources cannot be stretched adequately to meet these growing needs (Wuthnow, 1996). Adding to clergy woes is the fact that fixed costs—expenditures over which they have little control, such as maintenance of facilities and benefits and salaries for employees—are soaring (Hofheinz, 1993).

It is perplexing to consider the bust economy of the 1990s and the fabled wealth of the baby boomers, neither of which squares with the angst and melancholy reported in Wuthnow's study. With such plenty, how can there be so much want? And perhaps the most critical question is, How are religious leaders to respond?

The answer to the dilemma may be rooted in changing demographics, and the experience or the history of giving. In an address to the National Catholic Stewardship Council, Fred Hofheinz, senior program officer for religion at the Lilly Endowment, a major funder of research on religion, reflects that we are experiencing the "signs of the times" and that the impact of rapidly changing demographics is both a threat and an opportunity for religious leaders (Hofheinz, 1993, p. 522).

The changing role of women

Perhaps the most dramatic shift—one that has truly rocked religious organizations—is the radically changing role of women in society. Historically, the workforce of religious organizations was composed of women as either unpaid lay volunteers or as religious women who were paid very little for their labor because it was their "calling" to teach or to care for the needy (Oates, 1990). The authors spoke with a number of women, lay and religious, who believe that their formal and informal influence has positively affected the fundraising efforts of their chosen religious organizations. They attributed this to the dollars they have given, the boards on which they have served, and the advice they have shared.

Many of these women have multiple life responsibilities, which include a host of family, professional, personal, and community commitments. Today, 55 percent of American women work (*The Economist*, 1996). Thus, there are fewer women who can work as volunteers full-time, and fewer women are drawn to religious vocation and church work (Hofheinz, 1993).

Women now control 86 percent of the aggregate personal wealth in the United States (Larson, 1996). In other words, women, because of their family ties and spousal connections, legally hold certain assets, sometimes in their own names or in conjunction with their spouses. This combination is what is meant by aggregate wealth. So how did this staggering statistic come to be, and how does it affect the financial state of charities? The answers are simple, but they also engender a host of complex consequences that can spell threat or promise for religious organizations.

Biology is one factor. Women live longer and many wives outlive their husbands, thus they often end up controlling many assets and investments. Yet the numbers can be misleading. The disproportion of wealth is extreme, and the reality is that nearly 75 percent of all elderly women live below the poverty line (Larson, 1996).

Socioeconomic factors supply another paradox. More women control financial decisions, but there is often less individual wealth to control. The number of single-parent households run by women has increased, but they have less personal wealth than men (Brimelow, 1996). In two-career families, it is the women who make the financial decisions (Larson, 1996). However, the effect of the dual-career family trend fuels inequalities among family incomes. Women earning higher incomes tend to be well educated and tend to marry men with similar characteristics. This group accounts for most of the wealth. These women are more likely to keep their jobs, while some research suggests that women married to low-income-earning men generally do not stay in the workforce. Salaries of married, low-income women rise more slowly. The result is a great gap between the top and bottom of the range of family incomes (*The Economist*, 1996). Because low-income, not high-income families tend to support religious causes, lack of growth in the salaries of low-income families can account for some of the erosion of market share experienced by religious organizations reported in *Giving USA*.

A second seismic demographic shift affecting religious organizations is the aging and accompanying affluence of the baby boomer generation. It must be noted that religious giving is almost exclusively by individuals and is thus very affected by political, social, and economic trends. The January 1998 issue of *Bulletin* finds that "self interest is increasingly important to donors, particularly baby boomers. They are less interested in general, unrestricted support of institutions and more interested in designating their gift for a precise purpose" (p. 1).

The esteemed status of religion among charities is well deserved. For decades, religious organizations have served the needy and have done so with dignity, compassion, and grace. The impact of faith-based charities on American society is beyond measure. Indeed, religious social action exists at the core of social policy at home and abroad (Hofheinz, 1993). Opportunities for philanthropy abound, especially in light of the new welfare reform act. The case for religion to continue to receive the lion's share of private donations can and must be made, and women as fundraisers can assist in this area. Hofheinz cites another Lilly Endowment study conducted by John and Sylvia Ronsvalle that concluded that the "charitable impulse is directly influenced by affiliation with a religious institution" (p. 523).

The historical influence of women in religious philanthropy

Our position is that leaders of religious organizations have an unprecedented opportunity to tap into American affluence by reaching out to American women and offering them significant membership opportunities and voice in church organizations. It is also the position of the authors that women can claim some of their own power as leaders in society by seeking out and embracing these opportunities on their own.

As reported in *The Chronicle of Philanthropy*, July 10, 1997, "Many more women have the resources to give generously, but have yet to flex philanthropic muscle and fully claim the power of the purse" (Hall, p. 1). The article asserts that women are more likely to be found on committees planning galas and other special events than on foundation and charity boards making serious decisions about money and policy. Ironically, this was not always the case. The role women played historically in philanthropy, especially charities based in the Judeo-Christian tradition, has been curiously understated and overlooked (Deacon, 1996; Oates, 1990).

Early in the nineteenth century when the United States entered the Industrial Revolution, the predominantly agrarian life most of its citizens knew disappeared. As the population grew and cities developed, social and economic conditions changed rapidly and radically. Furthermore, throughout most of this period clergy were in short supply (Oates, 1990). Pastors could barely meet the parochial and sacramental needs of their parishioners. They had little time or resources to address burgeoning social exigency. This situation called forth a new legion of women, both religious and lay, who responded to the dearth of clergy and mounting social concerns with energy fueled by deep religious conviction. They were faithful women of means and service, and they were willing to help alleviate the suffering they observed.

During the period from 1820 to 1920, women—both religious and lay women—were the catalysts for many philanthropic efforts. These women can be categorized into two groups. One group was characterized by the educated and affluent matron who had the vision and the means to see a need and promote a solution. The other category consisted predominantly of immigrants—working-class and middle-class Christian women—who united in religious congregations or female benevolent associations (Oates, 1990).

A major aim for the working-class and middle-class women was to ameliorate the conditions of poverty throughout the United

States. During the nineteenth century much of the agenda for social change was driven by women. These women used a hands-on and collaborative approach to promote charitable causes and philanthropic efforts (Oates, 1990).

The middle- and upper-class women had the financial resources to supply monetary support and direction for the building of programs, physical facilities, and important relationships and contacts with people of power and authority. They were not reticent about assessing a need and acting on it. Like their male counterparts of this era, these women were able to underwrite programs favored by religious orders and bishops. This kind of generosity earned them a certain amount of notoriety as well as some papal accolades. It was not uncommon for elderly widowed women of wealth to leave their estates to religious orders on the condition that the convent or order provide a place of dwelling for them until their death (Oates, 1990).

Neither was it unusual for some of these women to support unpopular causes of the day. They cleverly and successfully drew upon their wealth, education, and social standing to personally oversee programs and projects that advanced the welfare of African and Native Americans. These women were raised with a social conscience and the belief that charity required a direct association with those in need. Their supposition was that such efforts would lead to a fairer and just world through social change.

While lay women were making their mark on society, religious organizations of women were creating their own remarkable story—sometimes in unison with their lay sisters. Not only did they play a major role by providing an incredible labor force, especially in Roman Catholic charities, their activities created many worthy agencies that became complex and prosperous organizations (Deacon, 1996; Oates, 1990). Social service agencies, schools, and hospitals are a few examples.

Given the social mores of the era, women eschewed management roles, appearing to prefer the more hands-on, mission-oriented roles of direct service to the poor. Leaving the governing of these major philanthropic enterprises to men, these women obscured the very powerful role they played in forging the American social conscience (Oates, 1990).

Women as leaders in philanthropy

The role of women in religious organizations has radically shifted over the last century and a half, and so has the role of women in society. Much of the angst religious leaders now experience is related to the fact that the large volunteer labor force has evaporated—women have migrated into the workforce and now account for more than 50 percent of working Americans.

Thus, as Hofheinz (1993) stated in his address to Catholic fundraisers, religious leaders along with other issues must re-think the churches' orientation to women. Women need a voice and a venue to be heard, especially but not limited to issues that concern and affect them. Church organizations need structures that are open to and encouraging of women.

In examining the history of the Catholic philanthropic tradition in America, Oates (1990) notes that charities became bureaucracies and as such, opportunities for a hands-on involvement decreased. At this point in history, many women founders became disenfranchised from the charity they had helped organize.

Active participation on boards is a vital way for individuals, especially women, to influence faith-based philanthropy and positive social change. Himes (1996) supports this view by suggesting that participation is an essential component of philanthropy and advocates church structures that invite participation. Vincent Cushing, president of the Washington Theological Union for twenty-three years, describes governing boards as the "DNA" of an organization. Boards in most organizations have power and through their decision-making capacity provide an opportunity to articulate their mission and values (Chairt, Holland, and Taylor, 1991). Simply stated, boards give individuals voice in the organization and the capability to exert influence.

Maddie Levitt, a philanthropist and fundraiser, noted that "money talks" when asked about women and board memberships. She continued, "Men have understood for years their power to bring about change—or maintain the status quo" (Hall, 1997, p. 22).

Martha Taylor, founder of the Women's Institute in Madison, Wisconsin, also believes that women need to learn more about how they can influence society with their material gifts as well as their intellectual and educational talents. As one tool, she has developed the idea of a speakers' circuit that draws on the skills of more experienced women who can help further encourage the talents of less experienced, yet capable and thoughtful women.

Women of faith will not only be able to influence the general welfare of our society through thoughtful philanthropy, like the women of the previous century described here, but they will also be in a position to change the religious organizations to which they belong.

We think the best way to re-engage women in the work of charities and to invite their financial investment is to actively seek their participation in the governing bodies of religious organizations. Women must be asked to participate, and they must be willing to accept such offers when they are presented. It is at the board level that dialogue can take place. Because they have economic clout, women can voice their concerns and be heard.

The opportunity to reclaim that valuable voice and presence of women in the religious philanthropic arena has never been greater. The economic sovereignty of women opens the door for women to be considered for membership on the governing boards of large religious charities and organizations (Shaw and Taylor, 1995). Although economic wealth is no guarantee of happiness, success, or life satisfaction, it does seem to promote significant influence and power in the philanthropic arena.

References

Brimelow, P. "The Glass Floor." *Forbes*, 1996, *158* (14), 47.

Chairt, R. P., Holland, T. P., and Taylor, B. E. *The Effective Board of Trustees.* New York: Macmillan, 1991.

Deacon, F. "More Than Just a Shoe String and a Prayer: How Women Religious Helped Finance the Nineteenth Century Social Fabric." *U.S. Catholic Historian*, 1996, *14*, 67–89.

The Economist, June 8, 1996, *339* (7969), 27–32.

Giving USA 1997. New York: American Association of Fund-Raising Counsel Trust for Philanthropy, 1997.

Hall, H. "Cultivating Philanthropy by Women." *Chronicle of Philanthropy*, July 10, 1997, pp. 20–23.

Himes, K. "Reflections on Financial Stewardship." *New Theology Review*, 1996, *9* (4), 52–70.

Hofheinz, F. "Catholic Giving and the Sign of the Times." *Origins*, 1993, *22*, 520–523.

Larson, E. "U.S. Women Have Vast Wealth, but Sometimes Lack Goals." Knight Ridder/Tribune News Service, May 13, 1996, pp. 513–523.

Newport, F., and Saad, L. "Religious Faith Is Widespread but Many Skip Church." Gallup Poll. [http://www/gallup.com/pll/news/970329.html]. 1998.

Oates, M. J. "The Role of Laywomen in American Catholic Philanthropy." *U.S. Catholic Historian*, Summer 1990, *9*, 249–260.

Shaw, S. C., and Taylor, M. A. *Reinventing Fundraising: Realizing the Potential of Women's Philanthropy.* San Francisco: Jossey-Bass, 1995.

Wuthnow, R. "Stewardship: The Cultural Context." *New Theology Review*, 1996, *9* (4), 71–84.

Wuthnow, R. "Churches' Financial Woes: A Crisis of the Spirit." *Chronicle of Philanthropy*, Oct. 2, 1997, p. 45.

JENNIFER M. GOINS *is vice president for institutional advancement at the Washington Theological Union in Washington, D.C.*

JANETTE E. MCDONALD *is director of annual programs at the Washington Theological Union.*

The YWCA of Columbus, Ohio, structured a capital campaign that succeeded through an innovative partnership of women leaders.

6

Focus on the future: A partnership of women in the campaign to renovate the YWCA of Columbus, Ohio

Karen Schwarzwalder

IN 1996, THE YWCA of Columbus, Ohio, completed the renovation of its landmark headquarters facility, the Griswold Building. The $15 million project took more than a decade to conceptualize and plan and more than four years to execute. It required a massive fundraising effort by the YWCA board, staff, and volunteers and a multifaceted funding plan involving both public and private participants.

The completed project houses 102 low-income women and space for the YWCA's administrative offices and program centers. The program centers include a child care center for physically and mentally challenged preschoolers, a center for school-aged children, a full-scale health and fitness center with a swimming pool, a health resource center, an auditorium, and meeting rooms. The renovated building makes a strong positive statement about the value Columbus places on the position of women in the community.

This chapter describes the YWCA of Columbus and the processes that the organization followed in giving birth to this project. It outlines the activities leading up to the construction project, including

NEW DIRECTIONS FOR PHILANTHROPIC FUNDRAISING, NO. 19, SPRING 1998 © JOSSEY-BASS PUBLISHERS

a description of the unique involvement of women as volunteers in project guidance and implementation. It also discusses campaign leadership, the challenges of this type of project for a nonprofit, and community participation in the fundraising. As CEO of the YWCA during the execution of the campaign, my role encompassed a multitude of fundraising tasks, as well as serving as chief liaison to the campaign leadership committee.

History of the YWCA project

The YWCA is a multifaceted membership organization that has operated in Columbus since 1886. Its mission is *the empowerment of women and the elimination of racism.* The YWCA of Columbus attempts to provide services to its members as well as to meet critical, unmet community needs that affect women and their families.

Since 1886, the YWCA has owned and operated several different downtown headquarters buildings, the most recently constructed being the Griswold Building. The Griswold Building was built in 1928, its construction having been made possible by a bequest in 1924 from the estate of Mary J. Griswold, the widow of a Columbus real estate tycoon. It is a 130,000-square-foot building, with eight levels above ground and three levels below ground. The top four floors were constructed as a residence for women. The remaining floors were designed for meeting space and for offices—both for the YWCA and for other organizations—and for programmatic purposes such as a fitness facility and a youth activities center.

The YWCA of Columbus has been important to the lives of countless people since it began in 1886 as a safe haven for young women leaving their family homes in rural communities to find work opportunities in Columbus. As the years passed, the YWCA grew in response to the needs of these and other women. Child care, job training and readiness services, health programs, war support efforts, assimilation programs for foreign-born women, teen programs, and educational and leadership development programs have all taken place at the YWCA.

Pivotal years: 1970–1989

The roots of today's construction project can be found in the difficult experiences of the 1970s. The association lost membership, and the community questioned the purpose and the relevance of the organization as programs declined in number and participation.

In the late 1970s, the board and staff completed a strategic plan. Called the Total Association Plan (TAP), this plan provided a guide and frame of reference for the entire decade of the 1980s. During that decade, the board and staff began to revitalize the program offerings and to place more strict controls on budget and expenditures. They completed a small ($1 million) capital campaign to renovate the lobby, the ballroom, and the health and fitness center of the Griswold Building. At the end of the 1980s, the board developed a second strategic plan. This time a five-year plan was developed, again calling for new programmatic efforts and resource accountability. A major thrust of the plan was to raise the necessary funds to provide adequate facilities to house the YWCA programs.

Status of the Griswold Building

Since its construction in 1928, the Griswold Building had not received much renovation. A wing was added to the sixth and seventh floors of the residence in the early 1970s; this was remodeled in 1987. Boilers were replaced in 1986. And, as mentioned earlier, a small capital campaign in the early 1980s had raised enough funds to provide some cosmetic renovations. However, there had been no appreciable work on any of the mechanical or plumbing systems.

Long-time members reported that the building had begun to show signs of wear and tear during the 1950s and that these conditions continued into the 1990s. By then, the building was in very poor condition. Electrical supply was inadequate, heating was insufficient, and air conditioning was available only in parts of the building, mostly through inefficient, window air conditioners. Plumbing was a great problem; pipes, mostly embedded in and behind poured concrete walls, were breaking with regularity. Plumbing trucks were parked behind the building almost every day.

Capital campaign of 1994–95

In 1990, Celia Crossley, a member of the YWCA board of trustees and former board president, volunteered to lead a capital fund drive should the board choose to initiate one. During 1990 and 1991 she, the board chair, and I quietly approached community leaders to seek their opinions about the advisability of a capital fund drive. The view received was cautiously optimistic, but it was suggested that the drive not begin until 1993 or 1994.

Construction project planning

At the same time, the YWCA board formed a construction advisory committee (CAC). Making a positive statement about women's skills and abilities was an important part of the planning phases of the project, so the board selected only women to serve on this committee. The committee, chaired by Amy Kuhn, a lawyer and real estate appraiser, included architects, bankers, real estate professionals, and lawyers—all women who believed strongly in the goals of the YWCA. Most of these women served on the committee for the duration of the project.

During 1990 and 1991, the CAC helped the board evaluate its facility needs. The board considered the highest and best uses for the Griswold Building, as well as the advantages and disadvantages of selling the property and moving to another site. Eventually, with the encouragement of the city of Columbus, the board decided that it would renovate the Griswold Building and remain in the downtown community. Two factors tipped the scales in favor of renovation. One is the fact that the Griswold Building is historically significant. It is a solid structure with graceful, classical architecture worthy of preservation. It also is the only downtown Columbus building built, owned, and operated by a group of women.

The other motivator was the city of Columbus's interest in maintaining the YWCA residence for low-income women. The city promised to bring substantial financial resources to the renovation project so it could maintain the 102 housing units provided by the YWCA. (Ultimately, the city was the largest donor to the project, giving $2,000,000 in grants and loans toward the costs of renovating the residence.)

In 1992, the CAC screened and interviewed twenty-seven architectural firms and in September recommended Moody/Nolan to the board. Although the firm is not woman-owned, the two senior architects on the YWCA project were women. The firm is minority-owned, thus furthering the YWCA's mission of eliminating racism.

Moody/Nolan worked in two phases. Phase I lasted through March 1993, during which time it produced an architectural master plan and a project cost estimate of $15 million dollars. This master plan served as the basis for all fundraising, both public and private. (Phase II included final architectural detail drawings, which were completed by January 1994.)

Public funding component

Also in 1992, the board began to lay the groundwork for substantial public funding for the project by meeting with representatives of the city, county, and state and with staff of Ohio Capital Corporation for Housing (OCCH). OCCH is a state organization that develops low-income housing proposals that use the tax incentives provided by the Internal Revenue Service to encourage the development of low-income housing. An agreement with OCCH was negotiated and signed in 1993, after a board retreat. The public participation in the project, including tax credits and state, county, and city grants and loans, ultimately yielded nearly $8,000,000.

Board decision to proceed

During these years, the CAC developed the project on behalf of the board and kept the board informed of progress at intervals. By the end of 1993, the magnitude of the renovation project, both in size and complexity, became clear, and before proceeding further the CAC needed to be sure that the board was fully educated and fully committed. A retreat was held for the purpose of full discussion and to develop a context in which a fully informed decision could be made. It is important to note here that this would be among the largest projects in the history of Columbus ever undertaken by a human service provider and the largest in terms of dollars raised through private philanthropy. In order to be successful, the board had to understand and agree to participate in the complex legal structure required to access tax credits and to help raise $7 million in private donations.

After a lengthy retreat, the board agreed to move forward.

All-woman campaign leadership

Once this decision was made, the board worked quickly. By December 1993, the board had appointed a capital campaign steering committee, which had interviewed and recommended the hiring of a professional fundraising staff. Hodge Cramer, a fundraising consulting business owned by a male and female partnership, began to work on the campaign, and Michelle Cramer moved her offices on-site for the planning period and the duration of the major gifts component of the fundraising.

Among the first decisions made was the decision to establish an all-women campaign leadership. This was again a first for Columbus in that all previous fundraising campaigns were conducted by male-dominated leadership teams.

Celia Crossley was asked to chair the campaign steering committee on behalf of the YWCA board. She and the steering committee members believed that the selection of the right general chair for the campaign would be crucial to success, and all agreed that Abigail Wexner, wife of Leslie H. Wexner, chairman of The Limited, would be the ideal leader. Abigail Wexner was relatively new to Columbus. Prior to her marriage to Les Wexner in 1993, she had worked in New York City as an attorney.

Both Abigail and Leslie Wexner had a history of commitment to the YWCA. The Limited had been one of three principal corporate sponsors of the YWCA's Women of Achievement Luncheon every year since 1990. Leslie Wexner had attended each year, helping to honor the award winners, and they began to attend together after their marriage.

In January 1994, the steering committee invited Abigail Wexner to visit the YWCA and witness first-hand how difficult it was to meet current program needs in such dilapidated conditions. She spent a full day with staff and board members, touring the facility and observing programs being conducted in the facility. She saw the deteriorating conditions and the lack of contemporary amenities. After her visit, Ms. Wexner was not only in agreement with our need for a new work environment but she was appalled at the statement that the dilapidated facility made about the community's commitment to women.

She left the meeting with a promise to consider our request and provide us with an answer by April. In April, during the annual YWCA phonation fund drive, she called our offices and committed to help us raise $7,000,000 from the philanthropic community and pledged $1,000,000 toward that goal. Her public statement about her reason for agreeing to chair the campaign was that it was the "right thing to do."

Campaign cabinet

Under her leadership and with the help of Celia Crossley, we formed a fifty-woman campaign cabinet, which accepted responsibility for helping to raise the remaining $6,000,000 needed. Abigail Wexner chaired this cabinet, which met several times in her home. The women represented families of affluence in Franklin County—business and political leaders. It was a powerful group, well-positioned to raise these funds.

Community committee

Celia Crossley and her steering committee also determined that they wanted to raise a substantial number of pledges from members of the YWCA and the broader community. It appointed a final committee—the community committee—to take the leadership for this element of the campaign. Chaired by Teri Gehr, a young woman who was a member of the YWCA board, this committee agreed to raise funds from small businesses, minority- and woman-owned businesses, religious congregations, civic, union, and trade associations, past YWCA board members, YWCA members and friends, and the general public.

Campaign period

From June 1994 through August 1996, all committees worked to raise funds. The most intensive time period for major gifts was during the first eight months of the campaign, when we raised more than 70 percent of the funds needed. Abigail Wexner proved to be a remarkable leader. She was an extraordinary presence in the community, and her presence in our campaign elevated its prominence. It was never a question of whether or not a corporation was going to donate to the YWCA effort; it was a question of how much. It is clear that Abigail's leadership served to elevate the level of giving.

The community campaign did not begin until the spring of 1995, and it was buoyed by a $500,000 challenge grant from the Kresge Foundation. The most significant part of the community campaign was the sale of bricks and pavers in the *Peace and Justice Walkway* in front of the Griswold Building. It is a beautiful walkway that makes a statement about the variety of people who support the YWCA.

Chart of gifts

The following chart demonstrates the number, amount, and type of gifts received in the YWCA renovation.

Table 6.1. YWCA capital campaign commemoration categories

Amount	Corporate	Foundation	Organization	Government	Individual	Total
$1,000,000	1					1
$500,000–$999,999	4	1				5
$200,000–$499,999	2			1		3
$100,000–$199,999	7	4		1	1	13
$50,000–$99,999	5	3			1	9
$10,000–$49,999	17	4	2		10	33
$1,000–$99,999	32		6		126	164
Total	*68*	*12*	*8*	*2*	*138*	*228*

Reflections

Today, the YWCA of Columbus is a strong, vital organization operating out of a renovated facility that well represents both the organization and the position of women in Columbus. The capital campaign served both these purposes, and it established a solid footing upon which to build the YWCA of the future.

Upon reflection, a number of factors emerge as reasons this project worked well for the YWCA:

The project was fully in line with the YWCA's mission of empowering women. From its inception, the project demonstrated the abilities of the contemporary woman, and many donors made contributions simply because they wanted to be in support of a women's project. The fact that women were leading this project and that it would ultimately serve the needs of women enhanced the potential for success. Large numbers of women were involved at all levels. According to Celia Crossley, "Every time we hit a snag, a woman came along to solve the problem. No one I asked to help refused me. Many women volunteered to help without my having to ask them."

The board and staff were willing to be bold. Projects of this sort are risky for human service providers because they are different from what the organization is accustomed to doing on a regular basis. Most of the board and many of the members of the construction advisory committee had not dealt with a major renovation project. Major renovations are always full of surprises, and this one was no exception. Fortunately, the YWCA board was wise enough to hire highly skilled consulting staff, including an owner's representative who guided the construction project, thus minimizing exposure.

Further, the public funding mechanism on which this project is based is a complex one, and many boards would have been daunted by the legal and banking structure required to support the use of low-income-housing and historic-renovation tax credits. In all, three law firms were required to negotiate the partnership agreements for the limited partnership related to the tax credit financing, and five banks were needed to provide the construction and bridge loan financing. All this is beyond the normal purview and expectation of a board of a nonprofit corporation, and the women of the YWCA's board of trustees are to be credited for their willingness to proceed.

As CEO, the fundraising and construction activity consumed most of my time during the solicitation phase. I participated fully in all fundraising planning and decision making, supervised the development and production of all print and video materials, and was integral to all donor request meetings; thus I was not readily available to provide day-to-day leadership to the organization. Consequently, the staff was restructured, as was the management reporting system, because of this temporary shift in my responsibilities.

The public relations value of a successful campaign and a successful project cannot be minimized. The YWCA's standing in the community was enhanced through this achievement, and it is easier to raise funds for operating projects because of the success of this project.

The project demonstrates the value of having a long-range plan and long-term commitment of board and staff. This work in the mid-1990s could not have been done without the efforts of the YWCA board and staff of the early 1980s who developed the first strategic plan and took the first steps to turn the organization around. Many of the women who were part of those early boards were still involved in the efforts in the 1990s. In addition, throughout those two decades there were only two executive directors. This dedication and service provides the stability and long-term organizational memory needed to make steady progress toward a long-term goal.

Rather than being a deterrent, the size of the campaign and the magnitude of the project helped bring people to the table. At all levels, people knew they had to give more to ensure success. As Celia Crossley says, "The size of the campaign seemed daunting at first, but we knew that we had to do it, and we did!"

Focus on the Future energized and invigorated the organization.

It helped the community be more aware of the importance of YWCA programs and services, and it built partnerships with the corporate and civic community that will last beyond the life of the campaign. It also demonstrated decisively that women in Columbus could be quite effective fundraisers. The project is still the largest private fundraising achievement by a human service organization in the history of the city.

KAREN SCHWARZWALDER *is president and CEO of the YWCA of Columbus, Ohio, and currently serves as president of the board of education of the Columbus Public Schools.*

In fields such as philanthropy, fundraising, and volunteerism, being aware and respectful of differences is essential, but it means that we as individuals take risks with our identities while opening our minds and our hearts to change.

7

Why diversity matters

Margaret A. Hendricks

WHY DIVERSITY MATTERS is simple. Diversity, by definition, means that individuals are valued regardless of race, gender, age, cultural or ethnic heritage, socioeconomic capacity, or a multitude of other characteristics limiting a person's ability to exist or thrive. Diversity means that people reach beyond themselves to know others. "Achieving" diversity does not mean balancing numbers. Legislation is not necessarily required. Even altering basic identities is not needed. That diversity seems so difficult to achieve, to manage, or even to understand within organizations today remains a serious challenge in the workplaces of both nonprofits and for-profits alike.

Diversity matters, above all, because its presence in the workforce reflects that individuals have been given an opportunity to participate fully and pursue success. In certain fields such as philanthropy and volunteerism, understanding the elements and importance of diversity is essential. Because philanthropy and volunteerism stem from personal convictions and from a willingness to share for the benefit of others, creating diverse work environments is crucial.

NEW DIRECTIONS FOR PHILANTHROPIC FUNDRAISING, NO. 19, SPRING 1998 © JOSSEY-BASS PUBLISHERS

But do diversity and relationship building, beyond their political correctness, really matter? What price do they carry? Why is nurturing diversity in the fundraising workforce an act of courage?

Definition of diversity

Defining diversity goes far beyond the color of one's skin, beyond ethnicity or nationality, beyond age and physical or mental prowess, beyond gender, beyond professional or educational achievements, beyond any other categorical ways we group people. Defining diversity almost always involves the use of labels. A key barrier in realizing diversity in the workplace is the tendency for individuals or groups to label themselves and transfer those labels to others in society. If self-labeling is not understood, we miss the expression of value systems, philosophies, and behaviors. We ignore pathways to building relationships. We ignore communication channels that can create lasting bonds. Labels are often so subtle that they remain unheard or unarticulated, but they are frequently revealed in moments of fear or anger. Yet to ignore the existence of labeling may cause us to miss the mark in understanding why diversity matters—with each other, with staff, with donors or volunteers, in programs, and in expressions of gratitude or recognition.

Beyond labels is framing the issue of diversity. Given a set of categories, diversity probably exists in most workplaces. Too often, however, it is the obvious factors—the ones people can see, hear, read, or recognize in traditional terms. For instance, consider the labels "woman," "Native American," "physically challenged," "volunteer," or "manager." These are labels with observable characteristics and implied behaviors. Taking two people with the same labels does not guarantee compatibility, effective communication, shared values and vision, understanding, or mutually beneficial motivation. The differences among individuals go to the very heart of each person's being, heritage, and life's experiences—far deeper than labels can ever reflect. Can diversity be that simple?

Benefits of diversity

Diversity involves three factors:

1. We exist in a global environment each day, no matter where we live or work.
2. Diversity, however defined, enhances our abilities to problem-solve, negotiate, and interact with others if we identify and develop appropriate communication avenues and value each other's differences.
3. Diversity adds dimension and capacity to our own lives and existence.

Over the last fifty years, race, gender, ethnicity, cultural heritage, socioeconomic dynamics, and age have formed common bases for defining diversity. The initiatives employed to achieve or embrace diversity are many. Some have worked quite well if we simply look at history and statistics. Take, for example, the integration of our nation's schools, the higher workforce participation of women and minorities, the creation of English-as-a-second-language programs, and the globalization of trade and commerce.

One of the most pivotal ways diversity is achieved is through communication, not just populating a group with "minority" representation. To work in groups or to problem-solve when groups are diverse can be quite challenging until communication systems are established that allow people to bridge the differences in their understanding and expression of ideas or concepts. Consider gender differences in communication as one example. As women have become more widely involved in all levels of the workforce, much discussion and multitudes of training programs have been directed at understanding the gender differences that exist in communication styles, patterns, and opportunities. As women have entered management, attention has been given to understanding patterns of administration that differentiate them from men's ways of administering. We count the numbers of women and see progress in representation. Inevitably though, we do not achieve a "oneness"—enhanced working relationships or problem-solving advantages—until we consider and discuss, on a very personal level, the perspectives that shaped these individuals.

Adding to the layers of diversity (race, age, socioeconomic status, sexual orientation, cultural heritage or ethnicity, professional preparation, or whatever other labels we can contrive) that men or women individually represent, we have a real challenge when we form relationships that work for a shared purpose such as philanthropy or volunteerism. Have you ever tried solving a common problem or reaching a mutually agreed upon decision before you took the time to explore and articulate the differences existing among the problem solvers? If time is not invested to identify and process the differences among individuals or cultures or value systems, problems cannot be solved effectively. In fact, in some instances, more problems are created—problems like marginalizing. Problems are resolved when differences are acknowledged and shared, when multiple perspectives are valued, and when there is a willingness to hear all that is being expressed.

One illustration of this is the common perspective that women, by nature, tend to find sharing personal matters at some level a "natural instinct." Collaborating or networking tend to be other natural tendencies of women. When the number of women in any mix increases, the group often begins to practice different methods of problem solving and collaborating. Many might argue that there is nothing harder to manage than a group of women. I find this an interesting perspective. Women do tend to bring more than just business to the workplace and, by doing so, challenge the traditional functions and structure of the workplace. For example, flexible work schedules, day care, equitable pay, and broadened health plans have been the direct result of higher numbers of women in the workforce. And ultimately, others have benefited from these changes. The point here is that introducing any diverse population into an established mix affects the status quo—existing practices, communication channels, and outcomes.

The need to personalize and nurture, in many cases, has distinguished women's roles in philanthropy, volunteerism, and even management styles. Through these roles they tend to create a sense of community that reaches beyond simple jobs and traditional expectations. They are demanding; they expect their energies to be valued, their ideas to be heard, their concerns to be considered, and their presence to be appreciated. Because women by necessity fill multiple roles in their lives, their sense of prioritizing is keen. Through their activities they seek to expand *what is* to *what might be.*

Women bring a special touch and perspective to philanthropy, too. When women achieve financial independence and choose to become active philanthropists, they seek to make an impact through the use of their resources. Issues of diversity—and therefore inclusiveness—matter because these factors represent the channels that allow women to flow from one realm of their lives to another and find expression. Working with women as professional colleagues in philanthropy or as donors has given me a broader understanding of what diversity can mean and does promise.

Price of diversity

To speak of diversity often raises the specter that a dominant group must change its "sameness." The price for change is far-reaching. Nothing remains the same. Why diversity fails or seems destined for conflict rests on the assumption that simply by assimilating others who are different we have achieved diversity and that those admitted will conform to the attitudes and behaviors of the dominant group. What really happens is that the balance shifts, even with one token representative, because the interrelationships within the group alter to accommodate the newcomer. Consider the massive demographic shifts in majority populations being predicted by the year 2010. How will we who constitute today's majority (white America) react when we become a new minority? If we do not find the wisdom to coexist in a different balance or mix, the result will be conflict. If, on the other hand, we are among what might be called the emerging majorities, can we accept or accommodate the time it takes for the transference of power or assimilation to occur?

Assimilation takes time, and the price is high—in lost capacity, in dollars, in team effort—when the time factors and learning curves are not anticipated in a shifting population. Achieving diversity represents a population shift.

When I think of assimilation, I think of Larry. Larry is a black American. For all purposes, he works so naturally within a majority environment that he seems "just like" everybody else. One day a person on my staff said to Larry, "When I see you, I don't see color. I see you, and you are just like me." After a moment's reflection, Larry simply said, "Not to see my color is not to see me."

A second aspect of achieving diversity is fear. Fear of differences always challenges the majority. For those involved in managing relationships, moving beyond fear to the real excitement of individual differences and facilitating understanding among co-workers can be staggering in the amount of time, energy, and reassurance it takes. We have to work hard to change our basic desires for sameness. We have to take risks in learning how someone else is essentially different; that makes us vulnerable. The interesting factor is that "same" is never "same." Diversity cuts more deeply.

A lesson in labels

Labels, I believe, form the basis of understanding diversity. For me the most gripping lesson in labeling happened at the 1991 Summer Institute for Women in Higher Education held at Bryn Mawr College.

Our class had seventy-three women from across the United States and around the world, each of whom held or aspired to an executive position within her current organization or as a next step in professional development. There was diversity in traditional terms—eighteen African Americans, eight Hispanics, four Asians, three Native Americans, and forty Caucasians. We were all leaders chosen by our organizations to attend the institute. The cost for sending us was high, requiring an investment of $10,000 to $15,000 per individual. We arrived, feeling pride in who we were and what we might accomplish. Thus, our framework appeared to be shaped by similarities rather than differences.

The summer institute is an intense experience. Each day begins promptly at 8:00 A.M., involves a one-hour working lunch often with roundtable topics, reconvenes from 1:00 to 5:00 P.M., and then involves evening lectures, homework, or group activities related to the curriculum. The first day is much like any first day at college: moving into the dorms, unpacking, endless introductions, and a cocktail reception at the president's house. The official kickoff event follows: dinner, speakers, the class call to action, and the getting-acquainted exercises. A certain edge of anxiety exists as acknowledged leaders become freshmen once again, their past and present identities needing to be put aside and new identities established for the month ahead. The stated expectations for the month involve establishing a national mentoring network among classmates and all alumnae and developing new professional credentials or directions for the next five to twenty years of one's career. Positioning is evident, and just to watch or feel the group dynamics of the first day is worth the total price of admission.

For us, the Myers-Briggs Type Inventory formed the basis of the two-evening, get-acquainted activity: one night for individuals to take the Myers-Briggs test, another for individuals to be grouped according to their personality types and given a management problem to solve. To get a sense of these dynamics, imagine twenty-three women whose test classified them as extroverted, intuitive, thinking, and judging, or ENTJs—in Myers-Briggs terms, "recognized natural leaders"—trying to solve one problem. Anxiety levels and personal dynamics flared. Consider, too, the tensions that emerged during the first day of class when the focus was "Understanding and Achieving Diversity." Add to that the dynamics of 1991: affirmative action in full swing nationally, a sense of impending societal surge, and demographic rebalancing. *People of color* was the inclusive and politically correct term of the day. Our teacher Bobbi, an attorney specializing in affirmative action and representing the governor's staff in the state of Washington, challenged us to consider many controversial issues in managing diversity.

The week then started easily enough. Within our focus on implementing diversity, we busily took notes and listened. A growing sense of homogenization emerged, somehow implying that all we discussed or could implement might flow into some logical, easily applied set of rules for achieving and managing diversity. What happened next was less predictable. Barely had we finished our first hour when Annie, an African American faculty member from Carleton College in Minnesota, stood at her seat and in an angry voice proclaimed: "I object to your term *people of color*. I am an African American; I am a native of Georgia, therefore a Native American. I am a dark black woman. I am Christian. I am a faculty member—the only black member of an all-white college faculty. I object to the attitudes of administrators as they deal with faculty." Annie continued with her "I am's" for another series of labels. She ended by saying, "I am more than a person of color, and you need to know me as such."

An air of disbelief and discomfort prevailed; moments of silence followed, our leaders not knowing how to respond to this anger or how to proceed if the term *people of color* could not be used. After an extended wait another woman stood, noting that she too was an African American of mocha color and then defining herself in her terms. Then another and another, until all the African American women had spoken. But that did not end it. The Hispanics followed, noting each in her own way that she was Chicano or Latino or some other label, not just a person of color. Then came the Native Americans and the Asians and the Caucasians.

For the next two hours, women of many "diversities" spoke, labeling themselves in terms that defined their individualities and even their generations. In the course of it all, labels like Irish American, middle-aged, handicapped, lesbian, administrator, fundraiser, volunteer, visionary, catalyst, and so many more were introduced as ways that people define themselves. It was a crash course in behavioral sensitivity. By careful listening, we could discern how individuals prioritize their identities. No longer could we neatly package concepts like *cultural diversity* and *people of color*.

In the course of the testimonials we each also confronted two difficulties: (1) the struggle for how we label ourselves to ourselves and (2) the inherent and often unacknowledged prejudices or reactions we hold within our hearts and minds when we hear how others identify themselves. Had we stood among our peers or had the group been mixed (men and women), the lesson likely would not have occurred; too many inherent barriers of power, position, prestige, or socialization would have existed. Thank goodness for the wisdom of the leaders to just let it happen. Because it happened, we as a group moved successfully through the rest of the month meeting moments of crisis, resolving differences, and sharing a closeness and wisdom gained through candid and courageous discussion.

Understanding diversity

Achieving diversity takes courage. It means that individuals must acknowledge their own labels and identify those that others place upon themselves. Whether we are participants or managers of this process, we must take the time and muster the courage to delve into self-definitions so that we can move beyond initial labels to build mutually beneficial relationships.

In philanthropy, for instance, consider the label "donor." As fundraising professionals, people with this label are our "business." It is our challenge to encourage people to become donors, to manage the relationship and "grow their potential," and then nurture a sustained closeness and advocacy, both for the cause and for the donor. We are usually drawn to this field or succeed in it because we have good interpersonal skills, a caring and curious nature, and a talent for advocacy. Yet I wonder how near we come to endangering these relationships when we do not take the time to uncover donors' own labels or understand their cultural nuances.

In our current era of recognizing and cultivating women as philanthropists, some argue that women have always been philanthropists. Others, however, see this as an area of great opportunity. The danger of the label "philanthropist" is that it obscures other labels. Few people—men or women—are willing to label themselves as philanthropists. Age is another factor. Anyone who has dealt exclusively with women as donors sees significant differences among women of different generations, let alone cultures. Attitudes toward philanthropy differ; the focus of gifts is determined very differently; and the ownership of the gift is claimed differently. The most difficult challenge I have faced with female donors is encouraging them to give gifts in their own names. Yet, when they do and particularly if those gifts go to benefit other women, the sense of accomplishment and self-empowerment the donors demonstrate is inspiring to watch.

Not many years ago I worked with the Critical Difference for Women Program at The Ohio State University. Critical Difference was a fundraising effort focusing on three areas: scholarships for reentry women (aged twenty-five and older); grants for research on or about women; and professional development grants. Typical scholarship recipients were in their forties, had high GPAs, had a 95 percent rate of graduation, and majored in one of a variety of subjects at the undergraduate and graduate levels. The most successful fundraising efforts—a 1,900 percent increase over two years—came from women giving to other women. These women donors ranged from twenty-three to eighty-five years of age, represented all walks of life and various cultures, and loved naming their scholarships or grants in their own names. As we paired scholarship and grant recipients with donors, special mentoring relationships were created. A major corporate foundation gave $500,000 because its female leaders were so impressed with the women-to-women giving model.

My work, while stimulating and exciting, became complex and unsettling as I tried to build awareness within the university about the following: the great untapped potential for women's giving; the needs for the university to change processing rituals (how gifts from women were recorded and acknowledged; how women were listed on mailing or alumni databases; how women were evaluated on their giving potential; how women were recognized; and even how the program itself was regarded beyond being "that women's thing"), and the opportunity for moving women as volunteers and donors into major leadership roles. Many of these changes within the university are now occurring; women are being recognized for their potential and asked for their leadership. Still, I wonder how long it will take for women to be considered for their potential as individually and as naturally as men are considered.

My recent work at Cornell focused on volunteerism—specifically, how work, family, and midlife issues influence baby boomer volunteering. A national forum on the issues of contemporary volunteerism, one of the first of its kind, was held. The funding for this program came from a woman in her seventies who has spent her entire life as a homemaker, business confidante of her husband, and community volunteer. Her frustration at being called "just a volunteer," specifically as she was placed among professionals, led her to challenge her university to hold a national forum. Her use of wealth inspired action that has had a national impact.

The gifts of diversity

The gifts of diversity are many. They include expanded self-knowledge, comfort with differences, the sense of a world interrelated and interdependent, and a sense of friendships from which we can continue to grow and gain insights. Diversity transcends labels like "women as donors," but labels help us to learn. In fields such as philanthropy, fundraising, volunteerism, and the social services, being aware and respectful of differences is essential, but it means that we as individuals take risks with our identities while opening our minds and our hearts to change. In these roles we hold the power to grow closer to one another and educate and influence others to value diversity.

George Bernard Shaw once said, "The trouble with communication is that we assume communication is complete when others have heard or read what we have said." Mere coexistence does not imply understanding and acceptance. Diversity exists, it is essential, and it requires mutual understanding. Diversity enlarges our own existence and brings us to a deeper understanding of other human beings. The interesting thing is that the closer we become, the more sameness we find.

Diversity matters.

MARGARET A. HENDRICKS *is director of development at the College of Veterinary Medicine, Cornell University, and president of First Step, a fundraising consulting firm based in Ithaca, New York.*

In asking for gifts, you win some and you learn from the others. Here are ten fundamental commandments of fundraising.

8

Lessons from the campaign trail

Madelyn M. Levitt

AS A SEVENTY-THREE–YEAR-OLD woman, I have been a philanthropist, fundraiser, and volunteer for most of my adult life. In reflecting on the many years I have devoted time, attention, and support for the causes of higher education, I feel somewhat like Yogi Berra, the baseball legend, who once said, "When you come to a fork in the road, take it." In looking back to where I have been and the direction I now see my life taking, I hope sharing my experiences might help inspire others to realize their own philanthropic dreams and aspirations.

I was privileged to be born into a nurturing family that instilled in me at a very early age what philanthropy means: it behooves each of us to return more to our respective communities than we have taken. How well I recall my first experience as a fundraiser at the young age of eight when I was a member of a Girl Scout Brownie troop. Even then the spark of competitive spirit was apparent when I asked my father what it would take to sell the most cookies in the troop. His reply was straightforward and has remained with me all my life: "To be the best at whatever you strive for, one must always go that extra mile." My identity was forged, and life as a volunteer and fundraiser took off. I have since applied that maxim daily while

NEW DIRECTIONS FOR PHILANTHROPIC FUNDRAISING, NO. 19, SPRING 1998 © JOSSEY-BASS PUBLISHERS

attempting, through philanthropy, to improve the quality of life for those in my community and elsewhere.

I have learned, in the process, some lessons from the campaign trail that apply specifically to women. I was a product of a male-dominated generation and did not always feel comfortable in making philanthropic decisions. I consistently sought the approval of my spouse about how much I should contribute financially to various community needs, even though the funds were coming from my personal resources. During the years, in speaking to various women's groups throughout the country about philanthropy, I have discovered this is not unique. Despite the fact that many more women have great monetary resources today, there is still a strong reluctance on their part to open their wallets for worthwhile causes.

Ten years ago, it was the experience of divorce that changed my attitude permanently about personal finances and motivated me to take command of my own personal resources. While the last thing in the world I would advocate would be divorce, it is still a fact that, statistically, most women in America today will either be widowed or divorced during their lifetime. So it behooves women today to make some intelligent decisions regarding their philanthropic intentions. If we do not take the initiative, Uncle Sam will do it for us through taxation of our estates. And it would benefit development professionals immensely to assist women in making intelligent philanthropic decisions, to empower them as individuals who have worthy philanthropic goals, because indeed we do.

As my role in various fundraising initiatives expanded through the years, this has been demonstrated to me many times. One of the highlights of my volunteer-philanthropic life was being selected in 1989 to chair a $115 million, five-year fundraising effort for Drake University, a liberal arts college in Des Moines, Iowa. One of the most challenging rewards of that campaign was a project that I often reflect on. In the midst of the campaign, it suddenly occurred to me one day that most of the bricks and mortar projects of the campaign bore the names of men, and there were virtually no women among the major donor group. I called a few of my female friends and soon learned the reason they were not participants in the campaign as major donors: they simply had never been asked for either their volunteer time or financial commitment.

With that information, I organized a small cadre of women to assist in generating the necessary funds for renovating the oldest building on the Drake campus. The building, listed on the National Register of Historic Places, was considered by many to be the gem of the campus. It was with a great deal of pride and pleasure that the renovation was completed ahead of schedule in terms of the necessary funds. The entire cost of the project was covered by charitable gifts donated exclusively by women.

Recently, I was asked to chair my second consecutive national fundraising effort for the university—Campaign Drake. I could have easily responded to this latest request by the Drake board of governors with the rationale that at the age of seventy-three, I have earned my day in the sun. After some soul searching and conversations with a few friends and my family, I realized that the first Campaign for Drake, which I successfully chaired with the wonderful help of others, was, in reality, the initial phase of a challenge to permanently secure the financial status of the institution. There were viable needs that still required attention, and building the endowment was identified as the major task required to fulfill the vision of the trustees.

Our Campaign Drake has been launched with a goal of raising $190 million by May 31, 2002. I have every confidence that we have the ability and tenacity to not only reach the lofty goal we have established, but, I hope, to exceed it. As I join with others in proceeding through the leadership gift phase of Campaign Drake, I review on a regular basis the ten fundamental commandments of fundraising that I devised a few years ago. They have applications for both professionals and volunteers as they inspire donors to "reach for the stars."

1. *Enjoy your fundraising efforts, no matter who or what you are raising money for.* Carefully consider your passions and concerns, whether you are a philanthropist or development professional. Do you want to improve the quality of life for children? For the

elderly? Do you wish to be a champion for education? For the environment? Determine what "floats your boat," and then find organizations and programs that match your desires. Explore ways you can further that organization's aims (and your own) and get involved with your head and heart. Keep in mind at all times the positive impact of your work and always share your enthusiasm with others, from staff to volunteers to prospective donors.

In my efforts to advance the mission of higher education, I think often of my parents, who instilled in me a strong belief in the great value of education. At any moment in our lives we can all be stripped of our material possessions, but there is nothing on earth that can deprive us of the education we have earned. My parents were also long-time supporters of Drake University, the institution I've been deeply involved with. My father, for example, was a member of Drake's governing board. My parents' belief in education and their loyalty to Drake motivated me to become personally involved with the university. The encounters I've since experienced with students, faculty, staff, alumni, friends, and fellow board members (I, too, have become a member of Drake's board of governors) have further fueled my dedication to Drake. I believe in it completely, and I have learned that my efforts on the university's behalf do make a difference.

2. *Be sure the project you become involved with has a high degree of credibility.* I have been known as a risk taker throughout my life. However, I have never accepted a volunteer fundraising commitment that was even remotely lacking a high degree of credibility.

Learn as much as you can about the organization or effort you want to support philanthropically or professionally. Ask the hard questions before you commit your time, talent, and treasure; when others ask you those questions, you can answer with knowledge and confidence.

3. *Make your own commitment before calling on others.* As I contemplated my initial involvement to lead Drake's $115 million fundraising campaign, I was fully aware that the university's previous fundraising campaign had generated $25 million. The jump from that amount to what I was being challenged with took a great

deal of soul searching on my part. I knew that if indeed I were to raise the sights of the university's board members, I would first have to come up with a challenge that would raise the philanthropic sights of my colleagues. In just forty-five days, my first challenge of a personal gift of $2 million generated $26 million, more than had been raised in the entire previous campaign. [Editor's note: She ultimately donated $5 million to the campaign and traveled more than 350,000 miles to meet with alumni and friends of the university.]

The Campaign for Drake not only reached its goal of $115 million in 1993—one year ahead of its scheduled completion—but it exceeded the goal by generating a total of $131 million. Needless to say, it was a great boost to my morale when I learned that I was the first woman in the United States to chair a campaign for a coeducational university that succeeded in raising over $100 million. Far more than the personal satisfaction I derived from the campaign's extraordinary success was the knowledge that a woman can and must make a difference in a male-dominated world.

4. *You rarely get more than you ask for.* You only have one opportunity, so make the best of it. Good fundraisers, whether paid or volunteer, know how to think on their feet when soliciting prospective donors for their support. Combine that with another vital characteristic: be prepared. Do your homework on the donor, your organization, and the specific project you are asking the donor to support. Then present your plan with confidence, enthusiasm, and complete information, answering any questions or making notes to follow up on those you cannot answer. Never apologize for asking for a gift, and do not be embarrassed by the amount. Believe it: being asked for a major gift is flattering to the prospect. And very few, if any, major donors have suffered a severe change in lifestyle because of their philanthropy.

Don't expect the donor to make a decision at the meeting. Listen to his or her concerns, answer all questions, and make note of additional information the donor may request. Always leave something in the donor's hand, including information on the project, a breakdown of its costs, and the amount of the gift you are asking the donor to consider. The exception: if in the course of the meeting you realize you are under-asking and the donor's giving potential is much greater, do not share the amount of your gift request. Instead, assure the donor that you will send a gift request after your meeting.

Have a follow-up game plan in mind before you leave the meeting. In some cases, the donor will lay out the timetable for what should come next or will provide clues as to what he or she needs, such as additional information on the organization or the project. If the donor expresses at least some interest in supporting the project, you can introduce information on ways to make a charitable gift. Whatever it is, clearly communicate your next step to the prospective donor.

After the call, immediately send a letter thanking the donor for the visit and reaffirming your next step. If the donor requested additional information, include that with your thank-you letter. If assembling the information will take time, assure the donor you will send it within the week. Then do so. The old advice to strike while the iron is hot applies here. If you do not act quickly, another charitable organization will.

5. *Remember that you are working to benefit others, not yourself.* Too often fundraisers act as if they are asking for a handout. Remember your passions! You are doing more than asking others for their hard-earned dollars; you are asking them to put their hard-earned dollars to work for a worthy cause. Share your enthusiasm. Express to prospective donors the various and specific ways their contributions will have a positive impact.

6. *Never feel you need to apologize for your request.* When you believe in a project with your mind and heart, you have every reason to feel proud of your request. Again, the gifts you solicit will support worthwhile endeavors, not your own bank account.

7. *Always select the right person for the call. (It may not be you!)* In soliciting prospective donors, both paid staff members and volunteers who have already made a contribution, or combinations of these, can be effective "askers." Know your organization and know your prospective donors. What has worked for the organization in the past, and what has not? What is the nature of the project for

which you need funding? Who is the best spokesperson for the project, and would that person appeal to each prospective donor? Does someone at your organization command high respect in the community and, thus, could be a powerful motivator among donors? Does someone at your organization or on your governing board have a special relationship with a prospective donor?

As you evaluate these and other questions, consider who will make the prospective donor feel most comfortable—but not so comfortable that the donor does not take the request seriously. You want the person making the call to impress the prospective donor in a way that will make him or her say, "Gee, if this person is supporting this cause and asking me to, too, then I ought to consider it."

The ego of the prospective donor is most important, not the ego of the caller. A development officer who insists on making a call because he or she wants that prospect may have lost sight of the organization's best interests: who would appeal to the donor most effectively.

8. *"Thank you" is the most important phrase in a fundraiser's vocabulary.* Use it often. Need I say more?

9. *Do everything you can to know your prospect.* This means not only researching the donor's relationship with your organization but also understanding everything you can about his or her family, interests, financial ability, civic activities, even personality quirks.

That information will help you devise a call strategy (how you approach the prospective donor) and also establish a friendly relationship. Your knowledge that a prospective donor and her daughter, for example, are involved with Girl Scouts and related community service projects will give you clues on everything from choosing a gift project that would appeal to that prospective donor to preparing to make the call.

Your ability to learn about a prospective donor relies on some of the basics of effective fundraising: having the best record-keeping system possible; investing in good research staff and systems; and creating a central clearinghouse or information source on all the institution's fundraising activities. These are not easy tasks, but they are vital to maximizing your efforts to connect to donors.

Major donors require and deserve lots of care and attention. They give as they feel appreciated, involved, and attended to. The minute your organization takes them for granted, they may take their charitable dollars elsewhere.

10. *Never become discouraged.* What do you do if the prospective donor refuses to even consider your proposal? Again, learn to think on your feet. Is there some element of the plan the donor found offensive? Is he or she simply trying to downplay his or her ability to make a major gift? (You've done your homework on this, so you know the donor is able.) Is the donor looking for a way out? In any case, do not corner the donor; instead, ask him or her to think about your idea. Always leave the person with a lot of options.

If the prospective donor says the project just is not something he or she is interested in, you might offer to discuss another of your organization's projects you believe the prospective donor would find exciting. Or ask the donor to let you go back to the drawing board to find such a project.

In asking for major gifts, you win some and you learn from the others. Your prospective donor may have a spouse who is not enthusiastic about supporting your organization. You might catch the donor on a bad or hectic day. You win some, but you don't lose any; you simply defer them. Be persistent and be prepared. Even if the donor does not contribute to the proposal on the table, work to keep that person involved and informed. Cultivate the donor's interest and continue to learn more about him or her. Eventually you will find a project the donor cannot resist.

MADELYN M. LEVITT *is national chair of Campaign Drake, an effort to raise $190 million for Drake University in Des Moines, Iowa. She has held public relations and development positions at Mercy Hospital Medical Center, United Way of Central Iowa, and Iowa Lutheran Hospital. Recipient of numerous awards, she was recognized by the National Society of Fund Raising Executives as the 1995 Outstanding Philanthropist.*

Index

Back Issue/Subscription Order Form

Copy or detach and send to:

Jossey-Bass Inc., Publishers, 350 Sansome Street, San Francisco CA 94104-1342

Call or fax toll free!

Phone 888-378-2537 6AM-5PM PST; Fax 800-605-2665

Back issues: Please send me the following issues at $22 each

(Important: please include series initials and issue number, such as PF90)

1. PF _____

_____

_____

$ _____ Total for single issues

$ _____ Shipping charges (for single issues *only;* subscriptions are exempt from shipping charges): Up to $30, add $5^{50} • $30^{01}–$50, add $6^{50} $50^{01}–$75, add $7^{50} • $75^{01}–$100, add $9 • $100^{01}–$150, add $10 Over $150, call for shipping charge

Subscriptions   Please ❑ start   ❑ renew my subscription to *New Directions for Philanthropic Fundraising* for the year 19___ at the following rate:

❑ Individual $54   ❑ Institutional $90

NOTE: Subscriptions are quarterly, and are for the calendar year only. Subscriptions begin with the spring issue of the year indicated above. For shipping outside the U.S., please add $25.

$ _____ Total single issues and subscriptions (CA, IN, NJ, NY and DC residents, add sales tax for single issues. NY and DC residents must include shipping charges when calculating sales tax. NY and Canadian residents only, add sales tax for subscriptions)

❑ Payment enclosed (U.S. check or money order only)

❑ VISA, MC, AmEx, Discover Card #_____ Exp. date_____

Signature _____ Day phone _____

❑ Bill me (U.S. institutional orders only. Purchase order required)

Purchase order #_____

Name _____

Address _____

_____

_____

Phone_____ E-mail _____

For more information about Jossey-Bass Publishers, visit our Web site at:
www.josseybass.com   **PRIORITY CODE = ND1**